The Best Book of
PUNS

The Best Book of PUNS

Col. Art. Moger

Introduction by Bob Hope

A Citadel Press Book
Published by Carol Publishing Group

First Carol Publishing Group Edition 1992

A Citadel Press Book
Published by Carol Publishing Group
Citadel Press is a registered trademark of Carol Communications, Inc.

Editorial Offices: 600 Madison Avenue, New York, NY 10022
Sales & Distribution Offices: 120 Enterprise Avenue, Secaucus, NJ
In Canada: Canadian Manda Group, P.O. Box 920, Station U, Toronto,
Ontario, M8Z 5P9, Canada

Queries regarding rights and permissions should be addressed to:
Carol Publishing Group, 600 Madison Avenue, New York, NY 10022

Manufactured in the United States Of America
ISBN 0-8065-1097-8

Carol Publishing Group books are available at special discounts
for bulk purchases, for sales promotions, fund raising, or
educational purposes. Special editions can also be created to
specifications. For details contact: Special Sales Department,
Carol Publishing Group, 120 Enterprise Ave., Secaucus, NJ 07094

10 9 8 7 6 5 4 3

Library of Congress Cataloging-in-Publication Data

Moger, Art.
        The best book of   puns/ Art. Moger: introduction by Bob Hope.
        p.   cm.
        1. Puns and punning. I. Title.
        PN6231.P8M58   1988
        818'5402--dc 19   88-39931
                                                          CIP

Dedicated to my lovely wife, Dodo, whose idea this sequel is . . . and to the thousands of pundits and punsters who demanded a sequel to *The Complete Pun Book*, which continues to sell well and please a lot of people.

Special thanks to Bob Hope for his longtime friendship . . . and to my editor, Allan J. Wilson, of Citadel Press.

If I can remember so many puns,
With all the details that mold them,
Why can't I recall with equal skill,
How many times I've told them?

—The Author

The pun is the lowest form of humor—
especially when you don't think of it first.

—Oscar Levant

Table of Pun-tents

Preface

Puns—we've laughed and groaned at the same time, but few would deny that puns have always elicited some reaction from everybody. Even God reacted with a groan at what was probably the first pun ever spoken. When Eve tempted Adam with that infamous apple by asking him to at least taste it, Adam replied, "I'll bite." The historical, philosophical, religious, and moral implications of that first pun still reverberate today.

Chaucer wrote them, Shakespeare wrote them, and there seems no end to the current pundits penning them today. Bennet Cerf, Dorothy Parker, and Clifton Fadiman are probably the most famous modern pundits, and aficionados of the movies laugh at the rapid-fire puns shot through the Marx Brothers films.

The ancient Greeks took time out from their

experiments in democracy and research into geometry to appreciate the pun. While laying out the Parthenon on the Acropolis Hill, somebody, no doubt, fell in love with the architect's precise math and probably mumbled to his friends that he loved his wife, but "Oh Euclid."

We know that the Elizabethans became so overwhelmed by Shakespeare's puns that they threw him in jail. Perhaps that's why he was "bard on Avon."

Sometimes we wonder how Cleopatra ever did manage to find a snake with which to commit suicide. Apparently, she was trying to raise them in ancient Alexandria and had a difficult time getting them to reproduce. Finally she was told that it was difficult to get snakes to reproduce. After all, "they're adders, not multipliers."

We can go on and on, but you get the point, he said sharply. With no further ado, but before bidding you adieu—and speaking of bidding, you know what happened to President Kennedy, a lover of the game of bridge, when he was defeated after not being able to make his own contract. "Somebody finally set a president."

I have called this book *The Best Book of Puns* because I thought the greatest glory of the pun is not just the play on words, or the reversal of letters and words, or the near pronunciations, but the ridiculous building up to the equally outrageous PUNch line. My joy in hearing or reading puns is not only the pun itself at the end, but the linguistic gyrations of the story leading up to the PUNch line itself.

I've collected these over the past few years. Where

did they come from? Who knows? It's rare that anybody can claim to have invented a pun, they pass so
quickly into the public domain, and the same ones get
reprinted and recirculated every time a new collection
comes out. But these are my favorites.

If you've heard any of your own that you think
belong in a book like this, let me know. I shall be
pleased to add any to a future edition and give you
credit—not necessarily for having invented one, but for
having reported it. Puns are in the public domain; they
belong to all of us, at least those of us who will have
them, and should not be copyrighted by anybody.

Enjoy them, and I hope they cause you no undue
PUNishment.

Introduction

by Bob Hope

I've known Col. Art. Moger for most of my adult professional life. I remember him coming backstage when I played in vaudeville, with a sketch pad in hand, ready to draw pleasing caricatures of me and fellow entertainers for publication in magazines, newspapers, and motion picture press books. Notable were his pen and ink sketches of cast members and myself in Broadway's *Red, Hot and Blue,* with Jimmy Durante and Ethel Mermen.

More recently, I remember Art. as a press agent for Warner Brothers Pictures publicizing a new actress-singer, Doris Day, who accompanied me on a tour of twenty-five cities in twenty-three days, playing fairs and stadiums. It was Warner Brothers Pictures' idea to gain exposure for this hitherto unknown blonde singer-actress, born in Cincinnati, Ohio, as Doris Kappelhoff, who had sung with Les Brown and His Band of Renown. Les also traveled with me and Tim and Irene Ryan as part of my "act." Moger reminds me that I told him to minimize my personal publicity and aim it towards this little blonde singer "because someday she'll be a big star!" (How prophetic I was!) Her first motion picture, *Romance on the High Seas*, opened to critical acclaim, and the name "Doris Day" became a household byword as a result of the publicity on her personal appearances with me and my friends.

Thanks for the memory!

Colonel Moger went on to become one of the nation's most sought-after press agents for more than sixteen years at Warner Brothers Pictures and other major motion picture studios. He served with such celebrities as John Wayne, Bette Davis, Bill Holden, Doris Day, Robert Wagner, Alan Ladd, Ida Lupino, Alexis Smith, Mickey Rooney, Jimmy Cagney, Andy Griffith, Merv Griffin, Anne Baxter, Liberace, Milton Berle, Montgomery Clift, John Huston, Merv Griffin, Alfred Hitchcock, President John F. Kennedy, Harry S. Truman, Elizabeth Taylor (serving as her personal escort to the world premiere of *Giant*), Col. Jack L. Warner (president of Warner Brothers Pictures), Red Buttons, Danny Kaye, Rhonda Fleming, Michael Curtiz (Academy-Award-winning director), Burt Lancaster, Mervyn LeRoy, Dan O'Herlihy, Tab Hunter, Mike

Todd, the Marx Brothers, Janis Paige, Rita Hayworth, Patricia Hitchcock, Harry Belafonte, Jayne Mansfield, and scores of other Hollywood greats, near-greats, and in-grates.

Art. was best described by his fellow cartoonist-friend, the late Al Capp of *Li'l Abner* fame, who said, "I have known Art. Moger for thirty years. In that time, he has publicized public figures who haven't half the charm he has. He has tried to whomp up enthusiasm for comedians who aren't half as delightful as he is. He has beaten the drums for movies which seldom told stories comparable to those Art. could tell.

"In a town like Boston, whose public relations men seem to have learned their profession at embalming schools, Art. is an oasis. He has all the flair of the Hollywood guys, without their fawning fraudulence; has all the vitality of the New York guys without their noisy manners.

"I'm always glad to see Art. no matter how little quality the thing he's publicizing has. He has the quality that makes him a joy to see.

"And to read, I'll bet."

Amen! says I.

Art.'s new book is a follow-up to his very successful tome, *The Complete Pun Book*, which caught the fancy of pun-dits all over the world when it was published several years ago. (It is still a standard among punsters everywhere.) Like a good motion picture, one success begets another. That is why we have such titles as *Superman I, II, III, IV*, etc.; *Poltergeist I, II, III*, etc.; *Jaws I, II, III*, etc.; *Rocky I, II, III, IV*, etc.; *Death Wish I, II, III*, etc. The only anomaly is *Surf II*. (There

was never a *Surf I*.)

Actually, in retrospect, when I made those *Road* films with Bing Crosby and Dorothy Lamour, it was the beginning of the sequel films and could have been titled *Road I, II, III, IV*, etc. Instead we hired specialists who were called "road scholars," and they originated such titles as *The Road to Singapore* (1940), *The Road to Zanzibar* (1941), *The Road to Morocco* (1942), *The Road to Utopia* (1946), *The Road to Rio* (1948). Soon thereafter, my successful movie, *Paleface* (1948), with Jane Russell, was followed by a sequel, *Son of Paleface* (1952). (We could have solved thinking up a new title by dubbing it *Paleface II*.)

Everyone knows that punning is the lowest form of wit, but it takes a true punster like Moger to tell you why. "Because," he says, "the pun is the foundation of humor, the bedrock of the belly laugh. Oscar Levant said it best. 'A pun is the lowest form of wit, especially if you didn't say it first.'"

In this book, you'll find a hilarious abundance of pun-ishment for the millions who can't resist giving a word a twist . . . and ammunition for a million occasions from the theater, movie, and TV wags, from wits of Wall Street and Washington . . . the gems from poets and pun-dits, the crumbs from the bottom of the punning barrel, e.g.:

You know, of course, that the only way to tell the sex of a chromosome is to take down its genes.

Golf is like taxes. You drive hard to get to the green and wind up in the hole.

21

Introduction

A monastery in financial trouble decided to go into the fish-and-chips business to raise revenues. One night a customer knocked on the door and a monk answered. "Are you the fish friar?" the customer asked. "No," the robed figure replied. "I'm the chip monk."

Among other achievements, Colonel Moger has been called a "Bob Hope lookalike."

The book contains an aPUNdix, a PUNabridged dictionary, and a collection of the best—and worst—jokes in the world. Like the fortune-teller who loved her work, you'll have a ball! Start punning. Like the dog in the flea circus, you'll steal the show. This is a book you've got to love for the sheer pun of it. It will make you the laugh-of-the-party. It will surely grab you by the jocular vein!

But remember, he who laughs last, didn't get the joke in the first place!

One of my favorite puns deals with comedian Charley Smith, who with his partner Joe Smith went on to fame with "Doctor Kronkeit" skits after leaving "The Avon Comedy Hour." Some of their skits were incorporated into Neil Simon's *The Sunshine Boys*, for which George Burns won an Academy Award.

While confined to a hospital bed, Smith was visited by a friend who said to him, "You ought to sue Neil Simon for plagiarizing your life story."

Smith thought for a second and replied, "No. Neil didn't plagiarize my life story, he merely simon-ized it."

A little known fact about Moger's early upbringing reveals he worked for his father, who owned a big farm in Princeton, Massachusetts, where he bred bulls and shipped them all over the world. When his dad retired, he turned them all overt to Art., who became known as "the biggest bullshipper in the world." (No one has been able to match him since!)

In conclusion, Art., thanks for the memories.

The Best Book of
PUNS

Pun Contest Winners

Soon after the publication of the original *The Complete Pun Book*, editors at the Allentown (Pennsylvania) *Sunday Call-Chronicle* began running a contest soliciting puns from its readers. There were no megaprizes offered, merely autographed books by yours truly to the lucky winners, and a free lunch in the *Call-Chronicle* cafeteria. Here's what Randall Murray, of the *Call-Chronicle* staff wrote when the winners were chosen.

Our lives are filled with catchy first-letter abbreviations which allegedly make our language easier to endure.

Everyone knows SALT, ERA, TGIF, SNAFU, and their ilk. Now there is another one: TGTBBPFCIO. That, in our newsroom stands for "Thank Goodness That Blankety-Blank Pun-Fun Contest Is Over!"

Pun Contest Winners

And over it is, laid to a much-deserved rest. Its epitaph in the words of one overworked contest judge was, "Arghhh!"

We have a bunch of winners here, folks, ten of them to be exact. We also have a bunch of people out there in Lehigh Valley-land with a strange sense of humor. Puns seem to bring out the worst, the lingual ghoul, in many people. This contest was no exception.

The Pun Fun mailbox was littered with groaners, chortlers, stomach churners, a smattering of evil chucklers, a few blank starters. The response, 204 eligible entries and six latecomers, was surprisingly large. We frankly had not expected such a flood of alleged humor.

So much for subjective judgments. The top prize—TA DA—goes to William A. Boyer, Sr., of 31 South Seventeenth Street, Allentown. The lucky devil will receive, in addition to an autographed copy of Art. Moger's book, *The Complete Pun Book*, a free lunch at the *Call-Chronicle* cafeteria.

Not only does he get to dine where the elite meet to eat, but Mr. Boyer gets to chow down with at least one of our illustrious judges. Talk about basking in reflected glories.

The fate of the remaining nine winners is reminiscent of a remark attributed to W. C. Fields, wherein the first prize in some sort of competition was one week in Philadelphia. Second prize was two weeks in Philadelphia. These nine do not get a free lunch in the *Call-Chronicle* cafeteria, but each will receive a copy of Moger's book.

It was fun. We hope all of you who took time to send in entries enjoyed yourselves—sadists. Fortunately, for newspapermen, the cost of five-gallon jugs of Maalox is a tax-deductible item.

Maybe we'll do it again. Maybe when you can buy commercial tickets for flights to Jupiter, we'll do it again!

AND NOW THE CONTEST WINNERS

Abandon hope, all ye who proceed beyond these portals. If the Food and Drug Administration has jurisdiction over such afflictions as chronic(le) paronomasia (punning), this page should carry a banner caveat:

WARNING: The material contained on this page is or can be hazardous to one's mental and gastrointestinal processes. Those affected by this printed matter are advised to use the following antidote—total abstinence from puns, washed down with any acceptable antacid mixture.

Our top punster has a double-barreled entry. William S. Boyer, Sr., floored all three judges with the following two entries. In fact, we were really in a quandary over which would win when we realized they were from the same person.

Here's Boyer's prize-winning pun—

You have probably run into people who are forever counting things, like cars in a freight train or how many steps in stairs, etc. Well, there was a fellow in Wildwood, New Jersey, this summer while I was there who went down to the beach one day and sat there counting sea gulls, waves, pretty girls, anything.

So, as he was walking down the pier, he started counting the slits between the boards. When he got to the end, he fell off and drowned.

The moral of the story is "When you're out of slits, you're out of pier!"

Number Two from Mr. B. is as follows—

29

It seems there was an Arabian sheik who wanted to invest some of his wealth in the United States. So he hired a New York attorney named Harry Regardway to handle things for him here.

It turned out to be a very successful investment for the sheik, and he decided to remember the attorney in his will. When the sheik died, his heirs found that he had left Harry his harem.

In his will it said, "Give my broads to Regardway."

Keep going. You can't quit now! Here's a winner from fifteen-year-old Robert Harris III of 1340 Walnut Street, Allentown. It's a bad sign from one so young.

A frantic young woman rushed into Abe's Able Dry Cleaners and said to the man behind the counter, "Listen, I've got a terrible problem. I spilled ketchup on this dress, and I need it cleaned in two hours. Can you do it?"

"Sure," said the owner, "but tell me, why is there a hamburger emblem on the dress?"

"Well, you see," she replied, "a fast-food chain elected me Burger Queen of 1979. I have to wear that dress at my crowning ceremony in two hours. That's why I'm in a rush. Can you deliver it to me, Michelle Getty, at this address?" She handed him a card.

"OK, I'll take care of it," he said. As soon as the young woman left, Abe went to work on the dress. In an hour and a half, he was finished. As he was going out the door, one of his employees stopped him and asked how to clean a certain fabric.

"I can't talk now," Abe shouted. "I have to deliver the Getty's burger dress."

Keep going. It gets worse!

We like the originality of this long pun involving automotive terms from Kevin G. Bausman of 614 Alen

Drive, Emmaus, Pennsylvania.

Making puns about cars can drive people carzy. It seems you never exhaust the number available about cars. The numbers seems to be manifold. At times, so many will come to your mind that you can't a Ford to remain neutral in sharing them. In fact, it can become a regular pastime in which you can produce puns of premium quality.

Once your mind is in gear, you can't stop or reverse the trend. Your thoughts just keep accelerating. Suddenly, you're enGulfed with puns. Your mind shifts from its normal thinking and begins pumping away, wheeling and dealing in puns. Some people will try to muffle you. Others will grille you for more. Soon the transmission of puns becomes automatic. It becomes a standard part of your life. It won't be long until you have people who will be your fans and won't let you Dodge their requests for puns no matter how Mobil you are. They'll clutch at every word you say.

People may say it takes engine-uity to do puns about cars, but soon you get tired of it. After awhile you want to take a brake from it before you run out of gas. Hood ever believe you'd get such mileage from puns about cars? You could have fueled me!

Here's one from Sandra Malard of 170 Lakeside Road, Ardmore, Pennsylvania. It's esoteric and appeals to the literati in us all.

Show me an artist's rendering of a seventh-century ecclesiastical cart, and I'll show you a picture of Gregorian dray.

George L. Grim, of 18 North Parkway Road, Allentown—no relation, by the way, to *Sunday Call-Chronicle* Associate Editor and contest judge John F. Grim—dredges up this one.

31

The king's son was pushed into the mud. In order to discover the culprit, the king lined up all his dukes and counts and announced he would start chopping off heads until someone talked.

After the first count lost his head, the second count began to say, "Wait, I'll tell . . ." Chop. It was too late. He, too, lost his head.

The moral of this story is "Don't hatchet your counts before they chicken!"

You know that your society is tottering when women, normally bastions of good taste and restraint in things humorous, get into the act. Thanks to Joyce Leonard of 903 Franklin Street, Emmaus, for the following tale.

There once was a drummer who always felt lost in the crowded band. He was never first or last, always somewhere in between. One day he decided to try another line of employment and went to work nights for a tailor. His job was simply a mid-drummer's night seam.

Ireland has Belfast, the IRA, and instant potatoes to worry about. Now add to that list this awful pun from Jeffrey D. Miller of Zionsville, Pennsylvania. He entitled this work "All This and World War, Too?"

During World War II, the captured Allied agents of Stalag 15 were attempting yet another daring prison break. On this particular night, Major O'Roarke and Lieutenant Flanagan were chosen to try to cut their way out of the East Gate.

They were hard at work when the siren sounded, and the floodlights caught them in the act. As the German officer led them way, O'Roarke said, "We were so careful. How ever did you catch us?"

The German replied, "It's very simple. Somehow I can always tell when Irish spies are filing."

Pun Contest Winners

Morton Sher of 604 North Muhlenberg Street, Allentown, peppered the mailbox with a number of entries. This one made it.

Singer Helen Traubel was preparing for a part in an opera at the Met. She was slipping into a girdle when a drunk staggered into her dressing room. Outraged Helen threw a vase at his head and ordered him out.

In the men's room, moments later, the drunk turned to an attendant and said, "Nobody knows the Traubel I've seen."

Good puns don't have to be long and involved. They can be short and punchy. That's why we liked this entry from Metro Perhoni of 676 Princeton, Palmerton, Pennsylvania.

"Some gardeners turn their lights on in the evening so they can watch their phlox by night."

And now, last, but obviously not least—it is last because that's how we stacked the envelopes—comes this offering from Mrs. Fran Mouotob of 365 Spruce Street, Emmaus.

At a convention of egotistical chess players in Miami, the air conditioning failed, and they were told to sit in the hall where more air was circulating.

The manager of the hotel was heard to complain to an employee, "I'm so tired of listening to a bunch of chess nuts boasting in an open foyer!"

That's it. Those are the top—or bottom—ten entries for this year. All of us overworked, mentally drained judges thank all of you—I think—for taking the time and trouble to make some ripples in the pun pond. It was fun!

Moaners and Groaners

Then there was a circus acrobat who always had a chap on his shoulder

. . . and the detective who developed cluestrophobia

. . . and the hermit who was arrested for recluse driving

. . . and the girl who thought she had met the perfect sheik—until she found a Bedouin.

Mrs. Bigger had a baby who was bigger than she was because he was a little Bigger.

Anyone can have four hands by doubling his fists.

Sign on my auto repair shop— "May we have the next dents?" puns "Broadway Al" Comi, the outdoor hot-dog king.

Even worse than raining cats and dogs is hailing taxicabs.

"When a man marries, he gets sixteen wives—four richer, four poorer, four better, four worse," puns Barry Schulman, program director for WBZ-TV, Boston.

A woman is only a build in a girdled cage.

Mary Russo, the IRS expert, puns that after a client left the IRS office, he said to his lawyer, "That auditor huffed and puffed and blew my shelter down."

Headlines, pun-style—
New Computer Continues Its Reign Of Error
Students Without Measles Vaccination Spotted
Textbook Editor Has Appendix Removed

Scholarly Debate—feud for thought
Gossip—one who takes in rumors
Four-letter word—par for the coarse
Chronic complainer—the world according to carp

A Baileys Crossroads, Virginia, auto-upholstery shop distributor pun-per sticker reads—"We'd like to get our hands on your seat."

Moaners and Groaners

Seen on a slow-moving auto, "I brake for tailgaters," notes nurse Janet Lewis.

A pun-per sticker reads "Legalize Bingo. Keep Grandma off the Streets."

This warning appeared on a sports car—"The Keys Are on the Seat Next to the Doberman."

Some unassailable advice appears on the pun-per sticker "If Your Cup Runneth Over, Let Someone Else Runneth the Car."

Paul Harvey of radio fame puns this sticker on ABC-Radio—"I Work in the Department of Redundancy Department."

One woman to another in a supermarket, "Hi, Helen! Why I haven't seen you since hamburger was thirty-eight cents a pound!"

Puns Harriet M. Watson, director of communications at Reed College, Portland, Oregon, "The difference between a book and a bore is you can shut up a book."

"Professional football players often tell punters and place-kickers how soft their jobs are—it's just for the kicks," puns noted sports attorney Bob Woolf of Boston.

Probate Judge Edward Ginsburg of Boston punned to his wife, Julie, "Juries must never be satisfied with their verdicts. They're always returning them."

Lawyer Dick Blankstein puns to his wife, Beth, "It's difficult to buy lunch for Prague divorce attorneys. They're always asking for separate Czechs."

Sid Grossman offers this pun, as his wife, Frances, gleefully agrees with him. "A few weeks ago we had a bad meal at a new restaurant serving German food. The appetizer was terrible, and the wurst was yet to come."

Sy Yanoff, general manager and veep at WNEV-TV, Channel 4, Boston, tells about his wife and a visit to Honolulu a couple of years ago. They went to visit Pearl Harbor, had a couple of cocktails, and got bombed.

Scott Coppersmith showed a photo to his sister, Cathy, to prove his pun. A nearby carpet dealer advertises "The best floor show in town."

"A group of suburban obstetricians in a one-story office building have a sign in their window which reads 'We deliver,'" puns Bob King, veep at Walt Disney Studios, California.

"Sometimes life for a lens maker can be a real grind," puns Kurt Schleicher.

"A person who likes clean swimming conditions at the beach should swim when the ocean is tidy," puns Marvel Comics Veep and Creative Director Stan Lee, in California.

Moaners and Groaners

Rabbi Frank Waldorf of Temple Sinai in Brookline, Massachusetts, addressed his constituents as "Ladies and gentlemen of the Jewry."

Col. Harry Wheeler III of Chestnut Hill, Massachusetts, said to his wife, Anna Rae, "Sir Lancelot once had a bad dream about his horse. It was a knight mare."

Len Meyers of radio-salesmanship fame puns, "A new deep-dish pizza parlor opened in Boston with great expectations. However, the critics panned it."

"The favorite dessert of most carpenters and boxers is pound cake," says punster Ron Morris.

"Some friends of our are doing very well in a candy-producing venture. They're making a mint," puns agent Dick Rich.

Pundit Betzida Prieto of New York says, "People who go hang-gliding for the first time end up feeling soar all over."

Pun-tributions from pundits with their favorite puns—

From Patric Foley—"The owner of a hog-raising business in Pilget, Nebraska, called his company Oink, Inc."

Puns Suzanne Ringrose of New York, "You might call

the head of the bicycle manufacturers' association the spokesman of the industry."

Punster Harvey Gordon puns, "When young sportswriters start out in Chicago, they often cover Wrigley Field as Cub reporters."

New York's Sue Weinstein puns, "In Encino, California, there is a printing company called Jack Rabbit Press—Fast Reproductions."

Noted pundit Wendy Jacarone writes, "There was an actress who was hired for the lead in a play about Joan of Arc. However, she ended up getting fired."

Adds Sandra Maunello, "When it comes to buying groceries, actors are not prudent consumers. They prefer a small roll to a long loaf."

Puns Linda Jacobs from New York, "I met Rich Little in Las Vegas, and he made a good impression on me."

A clothing store in Traverse City, Michigan, called itself You Are Putting Me On, noted Col. Herb Brown, better known as BATMAN, an acronym for Big and Tall Men's Accessories and Notions, with a membership of fifteen hundred shops worldwide.

"In St. Louis one fast-food spot goes by the name of The First Federal Frank and Crust Company," puns Amy Sandler of Boston.

Yoram Solomon of New York puns, "They banned the movie *Ivanhoe* because patrons said it had too much Saxon violence."

Stockbroker Vinnie Musto of Josepthal and Company, Boston, punc-trificates, "About the only thing you can do on a shoestring anymore is trip!"

Brother-in-law J. Jesse Rosen of Brockton, Massachusetts, puns, "I saw a sign on a church bulletin board—Athiests are people with no invisible means of support."

"A hair transplant is reseeding for the receding," puns Stacey Lewis.

Col.-Dr. J. James Dineen, Jr., gathered his family consisting of wife, Connie, son, James III, daughter, Sarah, and quipped, "If there was any justice in this world, people would occasionally be allowed to fly over pigeons."

Fourteen-year-old Eric Watson asked his eleven-year-old brother, David, "What was the tow tuck trying to do in the auto race?" His answer was "Pull a fast one!"

Suzy Hayman announced to Stacey Lewis, "Doctor Papboolagoolah will see you now."
"Which doctor?" Stacey asked.
"Oh, no," Suzy quipped, "he's perfectly well qualified."

Moaners and Groaners

This sign was seen outside a custom-building company, according to builder Gerry Mandel of New York Will Build to Suit. Next door was a tailor's shop with this sign—Will Suit to Build.

"A slogan for famed cardiologist Dr.-Maj. Charles Boucher of Boston would be 'With all my heart,'" puns his secretary, Georgia Lezcano.

"A slogan for couturiers, 'In my fashion,' and for therapists, 'Unshrinkingly,'" puns Jamie Pine of New York.

Femme-Veep Maria Carayas of SFM Media Corporation, New York, contributed this pun from a *Portland* (Maine) *Press Herald* story about New York City's mayor declaring a water emergency. "Koch called individual conservation the single most important faucet of our anti-drought program."

From the desk of Herb Shmertz, that genial, affable Mobil Oil veep and author/PR genius, comes a tribute to the late Bennett Cerf, "the greatest of all punsters," with this gem. "A high-school dropout landed a job that takes a lot of guts. He puts strings on electric guitars."

Leigh Calmar of Hill, Holiday, Cosmopulos ad agency, Boston, says, "An eccentric bachelor passed away and left his nephew 403 clocks. The nephew is now busy winding up the estate."

Moaners and Groaners

"Malaprops could be called a form of punning," says John Sias, ABC-TV prexy. "Casey Stengel, the former manager of the New York Yankees, called to his rookies at a Florida training camp, 'Line up men, alphabetically according to height.' "

Nancy Goldberg of The Boston Company, Boston, puns, "Mincing your words makes it easier if you have to eat them later."

Lisa Jaeggin, control accountant, The Boston Company says, "When you cross a dog and a hen, you get a pooched egg."

Credit Col. George Karalekas of the Republican National Committee with "A shoplifter is a person with a gift for grab."

A quick tour of ABC-TV reveals some good punsters. Here's another one from prexy John Sias. "My wife and I visited a married couple, who are both psychiatrists, at their newly bought house. To make them feel at home, we brought them the perfect housewarming gift—an assortment of nuts."

Handsome Fred Pierce, ABC-TV veep, adds, "A number of eye doctors live to a ripe old age. They dilate!"

After attending the recent bar mitzvah of a Chinese thirteen-year-old, Mindy and Andrew Mandel of SFM Holiday Network couldn't forget the celebrant's speech.

"Today I am a MAN-darin!" (A fountain pen, please!)

"I know an internist who gives complete examinations to hundreds of patients every year. He considers December 31st as the end of his physical year," comments Dr. Edward Parkhurst, that noted urologist-punster of the Massachusetts General Hospital in Boston.

Puns Kim Sargent, "When someone came into the movie *The Swamp* and inquired about the whereabouts of some missing underwear, another actor asked the person to 'be brief.'"

Sheila Yassa adds her favorite pun. "Last weekend I spent three hours trimming the shrubs around my home. When I finished, I was bushed."

From Karen Stack—"When a woman buys hosiery, she does not want to get a run for her money."

Another pun comes from Sarah Goldstein. "At first there wasn't much action at the singles bar, but, later, things started picking up."

And Nicole Richter offers her favorite pun. "I know a roofer who claims he handles all types of jobs and uses this slogan—'We top them all.'"

Groucho Marx revealed that his mute brother, Harpo, rarely spoke, but when he did, you could hear a pun drop.

Soren P. West, Jr., puns, "The pro at my tennis club offered a special discount on lessons for the next three weeks. His bulletin board sign read 'First Come, First Serve.'"

Bob Sullivan, the noted librarian executive at the Brookline Public Library told me about the time he selected a title for a patron who asked for a critique of *Walden*. When the patron inquired whether the work was fairly comprehensive, Paul replied, "It looks pretty Thoreau to me."

A neighbor of mine, Fred Brodney, a stockbroker, brought home an old telephone booth for his basement. The phone didn't work, but it was quite a conversation piece.

Mike Selig of Fay Foto Services, Boston, puns that the camera is used extensively in various types of businesses. He says, "It lens itself to many uses."

Debbie Moger advised her husband, Bob, to "Carry an extra stick in your golf bag. You never know when you might get a hole in one."

Travel bureau expert Bob Parsons, of the America Program Lecture Bureau in Boston, an avid punster, tells about his wife, Elyse's, desire to open up a franchise to sell mobile homes in his town. "They'll call her a wheel estate broker," added Bob.

During recent snowstorms, my efficient former

secretary Joan (Mansfield) Brannigan noted that snowplow operators were very perceptive people. "They always get the drift of it."

"A union steward at an automobile plant was investigating a complaint that an employee was fired for taking a brake," moans General Manager/Veep Gerald Walsh, the head honcho at WLVI-TV, Boston.

Punster Ken Crystal of Crystal Shoes, Boston, brought home some flowers for his wife, Ann, and was shaking when he told her the florist had been held up by an armed robber. You might describe the man as a petrified florist.

Sickness comes in three stages—Ill, Pill, and Bill.

In the animal family—
Kangaroo—a pogo stick with a pouch
Armadillo—possum on the half shell
Porcupine—punk-rocker animal
Zebra—horse behind bars
Lion—preditor-in-chief
Horse—the difference between a wild one and a tame one is a bit

George Stevens, Jr., of the JFK Center for the Performing Arts, puns, "In my younger days when I was courting, I would invite her to my apartment to help me make hamburgers. Then I could tell everyone she was my grille friend."

"Tibet can well be the world's noisiest country. Everywhere you go, it's yak, yak, yak," puns Lori Ann Barries of SFM Holiday Networks

"There's a new book on cloning entitled *Duet Yourself*," adds Amy Saverteig of SFM Holiday Network, promotion head.

A customer visiting a house of ill repute in Bangkok referred to the girl who trussed him up as "the Thai that binds."

Squire Rushness of ABC puns, "I've just bought a country house. It has five rooms and a path."

A woman commenting on her friend's painful sunburn said, "She got what she basked for."

If you're thin, don't eat fast; if you're fat, don't eat—fast.

Window shopping is "eye browsing."

Howard Spiess of Marblehead, Massachusetts, advised his wife, Louise, "Don't park your mobile home on top of a hill. It can leave you if it is so inclined."

"When two cartoonists entered a contest, the result was destined to be a draw," puns cartoonist Paul Dondan to Bernice Weinstock.

"A football player who continues to play after he is

all washed up becomes a scrub," admits Rich Frank.

Ed Reilly admits that as soon as he entered his dentist's office for root canal work, he lost his nerve.

Many migrating birds view an empty birdhouse along the way as a cheep hotel.

"A shoe store owned by one person would be called a sole proprietorship," puns John Sousa of Brookline, MA.

A man who loves to be outside when it snows is called a flaky person.

Mike Weinblatt of New York says, "Money spent on detergent to unclog one's kitchen sink is money down the drain."

"A friend of mine is opening a series of weight-reducing salons on a big scale," puns Ray Timothy, exec-veep at NBC-TV.

Puns Mark Cohen of ABC to the waiter after a spicy Mexican meal with President Tom Leahy of CBS-TV, "Give my condiments to the chef."

Artie Rizzo of Boston's Park Plaza Hotel quips, "A good hotel employee is one who is inn-experienced."

John Fici of Boston puns to his wife, Dolly, "Two young women were strolling along Stuart Street late one evening. They noticed two young men following them. One said, 'Aren't you afraid those young men are out after hours?' The other replied, 'I certainly hope so!' "

Harold O. Kinsman noted that he knew two hypochondriacs who had a hurt-to-hurt conversation every time they met.

Bob Sage, the head of Sage Motor Hotels, Incorporated, once had a snake charmer and a mortician as guests at one of his Boston hotels. The couple brought their own towels, monogrammed with Hiss and Hearse.

Walter Staab and Bob Frank of SFM Media Services of New York noted that a Turkish nut dessert was tasty. "That's a halvah thing to say," admitted one of them.

Mrs. Harold Rosenberg of Arizona defines the word "coincide" as what one does when it starts to rain.

Athlete's foot comes from Athlete's feat!

Overheard in the dressing room of the Stout/Big Men's Shop, Boston, by salesman Joe Turco, "I see where a farmer in Pittsfield would rather contend with a small boll weevil than a large one because it's the lesser of two weevils."

Bow-tie wearer Earl Rosenberg, of the same establishment mentioned above, was a passenger on a train when he was awakened in the middle of the night to help deliver a baby in the sleeping compartment. Puns Earl, "It was in the upper birth."

My two books, *The Complete Pun Book* and *Hello! My Real Name Is . . .* were very popular in Boston. "You might say the books had MASS appeal," mused Walter Baclawski, also from the dressing rooms of the Stout/Big Men's Shop.

My pun-in-law, Walter S. Bernheimer II, submits his favorite pun. "Many people believe that legalized gambling has made Atlantic City a bettor place."

Just returned from the Orient, publisher-editor Paul J. Reale, of *New England Entertainment Digest*, defines a Chinese spy as a "Peiping Tom."

A woman used a glass diaphragm because she wanted a womb with a view.

Pun-ch Lines

"If you really want a down-to-earth mate, marry a gardener," comments Col. Harry Bookhalter of Boston to his wife Muriel.

"They say all sheep are alike—actually, they have mutton in common," says Col. Gerald R. Walsh, veep/GM at WLVI-TV, Boston.

NEUROTIC—"Someone who worries about things that didn't happen in the past instead of worrying about things that won't happen in the future," says Jack Thomas, TV editor, *Boston Globe*.

"Give some people enough rope and they'll hang you!" observes Arthur Rosenfield, ex-post office mail carrier.

A daydreaming student wanted to quit school to work in a factory making frozen orange juice. He didn't get the job because he couldn't concentrate.

Maybe the grass looks greener on the other side of the fence because they take care of it over there.

Skeletons study for tests by boning up on the facts.

"Don't you wish all those people trying to find themselves would get lost?" mutters Col. Paul Sullivan, TV editor, *Boston Herald*.

What goes Ho! Ho! Swoosh!? Santa stuck in a revolving door.

"If you're still trying to find yourself, it's time for a haircut," says Lois Combs, governor's office, State Capitol, Frankfort, Kentucky.

If you're ever thinking about doing drugs, don't. Remember what happened to Humpty Dumpty. He was killed by a pusher.

"A dog's best friend is her mutter," puns financial advisor Deborah Ann Bernheimer of Boston.

Teachers are United Mind Workers.

"The difference between a letter ready for posting

and a lady going along a road is one is addressed in an envelope and the other is enveloped in a dress," observes Col. Kenneth J. Gore, pharmaceutical sales manager at Otis Chapp Co., Canton, MA.

Seen on the wall of a high school—This Is a Mental Institution.

A witch primping for a big night out is sure to use a spritz of scare spray.

Be alert. After all, the world needs more lerts.

"A girl is like a mirror when she is a good-looking lass," puns David Town Watson, Portland, Oregon's champion soccer player.

One thing about free advice, it's usually worth it.

Rosalind Bernheimer, of Waban, Massachusetts, and a Bennington College graduate, notes, "Birds are melancholy in the morning because their little bills are over dew."

When Clark Gable was just starting out in Hollywood, his agent advised him to be a dreamboat, not a shipwreck.

Pun-ch Lines

What streets do ghosts live on?
Dead ends.

The difference between a cat and a comma is that a cat has its claw at the end of its paws, and a comma has its pause at the end of a clause," puns Andy Bernheimer, hockey manager at Williams College, Williamstown, Massachusetts.

Students who spend half their time trying to be witty end up as half-wits.

Ever wonder how trains hear? Through their engineers, naturally.

A birthday cake made out of baked beans can blow out its own candles.

Read about a girl who was determined to let her hair grow out in bangs, so she ate TNT.

A turkey is a lot like a ghost when it's a-gobblin.

More Moaners and Groaners

Early Winter—Novemberrrrr.

"I've got a tooth that is driving me to extraction," quips Los Angeles movie mogul Mort Goldstein, punster.

Asked if he liked intellectual girls, Col. Jordan Ringel, lawyer-movie producer, replied, "I like a girl with a good head on my shoulder."

When asked why he left his last job, Col. David Savage, of Brookline, replied to his wife Avis. "Illness.

My boss got sick of me."

Speaking of his wife, Rhonda, Col. Arthur Katz, the billboard wizard, says, "Her face is her fortune—and it runs into a nice figure."

Speaking of an acquaintance, Agatha Dorfman of Newton, Massachusetts, said, "He hasn't an enemy in the world—but all his friends hate him!"

"Oh, well, accidents will happen," commented Captain Hook, offhandedly, notes Kathy Bernheimer of Wesleyan University.

STRICTLY SPEAKING

HALO—a greeting used by angels
ATROPHY—an award given to those who do not exercise
STEERING COMMITTEE—four people trying to park a car
STAMPEDE—a mad rush to the post office
EUROPE—next one to bat (Tricky?)

Typing isn*t bad, once you get the hangk ofit.

Adam and Eve lived appley ever after.

Chain smokers get rusty lungs.

Don't lend people money. It gives them amnesia.

"Some people's idea of curbing their appetites is to

park at a drive-in restaurant," puns comedian Bill Cosby.

Nothing you put into a banana split is as fattening as a spoon.

"Never choose a first mate who delights in taking the wind out of your sails," advised Jim Fiebig of NANA.

Jeffrey Gore, of Norwood, Massachusetts, notes, "A credit card is actually a 'buy pass.'"

UNUSUAL HEADLINES

Shipbuilders Launch New Contract Talks
Barbers Against Big Cut

"Second opinions are very popular these days. People think a second and then give you their opinions," notes TV's Johnny Carson.

Fact of life—People who snore always fall asleep fast.

"The only thing more powerful than the delirious joy of being number one is the humiliating disgrace of being number two," observes auto dealer-supreme, Herb Abramson of Wellesley, Massachusetts.

"Greed is an itch that resists all scratching," says Marty Ross of New York.

"Would you like your coffee black?" asked the waiter

of Robin Lyn Moger, producer's associate on "Ryan's Hope" at ABC-TV.

"What other colors do you have?" she asked.

"Anyone can have a second house, a second car, a second TV. All it takes is a second job, a second mortgage, and a second wind,"notes Mindy Mandel, SFM Entertainment's ace amanuensis in New York, as hubby Andrew grins.

"The Scots invented golf—which also might explain why they invented Scotch," noted Hon. Henry J. Stein of Brookline, as wife Fay snickers in delight.

"To err is human—but you better have a better excuse than that for the IRS," quips Gerry Eidelman, Brookline's ace accountant.

WHAT THIS COUNTRY NEEDS . . .

". . . more open minds and fewer open mouths.
". . . three presidents—one for the White House, one for traveling, and one to know what the people want.
". . . a supermarket cart with four wheels that point in the same direction."

—Sid Ascher, *Mainland Journal*,
Pleasantville, New Jersey

Toastmaster George Roberts observes, "My accountant is perfectly suited for his profession. He is five-feet-six-inches tall and $30,000 short."

More Moaners and Groaners

"An artist is someone to be feared when he draws a gun," notes Col/Adm. Stan Lee, creative director and veep at Marvel Productions, Van Nuys, California.

Commenting on a horror film, Sam Feldman, veep at National Amusement Corporation, Dedham, Massachusetts, observed, "Oh, how they loved each shudder."

Superadman Herb Manloveg of New York puns these two words—"Cucumber, a vegetable that's always in a pickle, and a Bore, someone who tells you a story from A to ZZZZ."

Giant's football fan Col. Joe Gerard, veep at SFM Entertainment, puns, "Life is like a shower. One wrong turn and you're in hot water."

Then there's the triple pun about a woman's three sons who went to Texas to raise beef cattle, sheep, and hogs. Stumped for a good name for their ranch, they wrote home to mother for suggestions. "Name it 'Focus,'" she telegraphed back. Puzzled, they wired for an explanation. The reply came immediately. "Focus, where the sun's rays meet." (Where the sons raise meat.)

Adm. Len Barrack and his wife, Col. Marge Roedig-Barrack, of Boston, pun, "Doing business without advertising is like winking in the dark. You know what you are doing, but no one else does."

"Another unhappy thought, maybe the graying isn't premature," observes Mike Sandler of Weston, Massachusetts, as his wife, Ellen, concurs.

"The narrower the mind, the broader the statement," puns Col. Sam Dame, United States Army, Retired, and lecture bureau tycoon of Boston's prestigious Lordly and Dame.

"Sheep get their haircuts at the baa baa shop," puns Jack Stein, the makeup king.

Magician Carl Bertolino of Boston puns, "Show me a person with a song in his heart, and I'll show you a man with an AM/FM pacemaker."

"Pandemonium is what you call deluxe housing for pandas," puns lovely Jessica Klempner of Beechwood, Ohio, as her two sisters, Stephanie and Rebecca, agree.

"Two words will win any argument. They are 'I agree,'" observes Matthew Katz of Lynnfield, Massachusetts, much to the chagrin of his brother, Jeffrey.

"A sugar-refining company executive travels overnight on business and stays in suites," puns hotel executive Greg Plank of Georgia.

Radio DJ Jess Cain of WHDH-Radio, Boston—its number-one rated radio personality—refers to busboys as "dish jockeys."

More Moaners and Groaners

"Once a person gets his barber's license, he will do his best to get ahead," puns orchestra leader Les Smith.

Comedian-malaprop expert Norm Crosby notes, "People in the monogram business achieve initial success."

"All publishers have books that are bound to do well," puns my publisher, Col. Allan J. Wilson of Citadel Press, Secaucus, New Jersey.

"The number of Americans who are overweight has reached nearly ninety million. That's in round figures, of course," writes Mrs. Eleanor Stearns of Newton, an Esther Williams lookalike.

Sign on a health-food restaurant, "All you should eat—$3," seen by Col. John A. Verrengia, controller at the Sage Motor Hotels, Boston.

Seen at a German restaurant, "Where the in-kraut goes to eat," by Steve Ganak, head of Steve Ganak Ad Reps, Boston.

And seen by Eric Lange, Steve's associate, "We're number one on the best-cellar list," at an inn's wine racks.

My friend Ira Kleinerman of New York has bank accounts all labeled I.R.A. accounts.

"College students from the Republic of China don't

get drunk very often, but once in a while they like to Taiwan on," says world traveler Corinne Dame of Dame Associates of Boston.

"When a man jumped off the Eiffel Tower with a parachute and landed in the river, they declared the man in Seine," says adman-author Ray Barron of Boston.

When President-Col. Paul R. Del Rossi of General Cinema Corporation met his wife and went shopping and lunched at Marshall Field and Company, you might say they had a Field day, notes his secretary, Janet O'Malley.

HEIR CONDITIONED

Heir filter	last will and testament
Heir fare	executor's fee
Heir cut	disinheritance

"At one time, there was a Sea Scout camp outside of Norfolk, Virginia, that was so close to the beach, the porpoises used to swim into shore at dinnertime. The camp's chef would announce the meal by yelling, 'Chow time! For all in tents and porpoises!'" puns John R. Crosbie.

CATCH PHRASES

Stewardess	"It was love at first flight."
Cabdriver	"You're my fare, lady."

Contortionist	"Head over heels."
Feminist	"Be my equal"
Pantomimist	"Please say you'll be mime."

"I know a fellow who is called a big thinker—by people who lisp," notes David LaCatnera of the Lordly and Dame, Inc., Boston, MA.

Eugene Harris, of Boston, Steve's assistant, adds, "I know a girl who lost 150 pounds recently. Her husband left her!"

KNOCK KNOCKS

Knock, knock.
Who's there?
Domino.
Domino who?
Domino cowhand, puns Holly Coleman.

Knock, knock.
Who's there?
Butcher.
Butcher who?
Butcher arms around me, honey, and hold me tight, puns Roth Hollingsworth.

Knock, knock.
Who's there?
Frankfurter.
Frankfurter who.
Frankfurter memories, puns Alex Langlois.

"At school I learned the three 'Rs'—Rah! Rah! Rah!" notes pundit Ellen Dunne.

One of the earliest and most popular forms of puns are "knock knocks." My teen-aged granddaughter, Jill Bernheimer, collected some "gems" from classmates and friends at Milton Academy. (See above.)

Football pundits will appreciate the nicknaming of their favorite professional football teams during the 1987 NFL strike when management brought in substitute players. The new names for these less-than-adequate teams appeared in the Boston *Globe* and was submitted by Dr. Peter Town Watson, of Portland, Oregon—the New England ex-Patriots, the Philadelphia Illegals, Los Angeles Lilliputians, New York Jests, Cincinnati Bengullibles, Tampa Bay Half-A-Bucs, Pittsburgh Stealers, Buffalo Counterfeit Bills, Los Angeles Lambs, Chicago Bad News Bears, and Detoit Lyins.

Hon. Martin Linsky, political expert and professor at the John F. Kennedy School of Public Affairs at Harvard University, sends along this worthy pun from the Dallas *News.* "During the gala, the Bushes shared the spotlight with such Texas luminaries as Lynda Johnson Robb and former Gov. John Connally and his wife, Nellie. The Connallys, in fact, generated the second-biggest ovation—behind the Bushes."

From a book review in the Plains, Georgia, *Monitor:* "*Margaret's Story*, Eugenia Price. A woman of virtue in the nineteenth century South. Fiction," puns artist Bernie Weinstock of Boston.

From an ad in the Hurst, Texas, *Mid-Cities Daily News*, "LOST: small apricot poodle, reward, neutered like one of the family."

From the church-news section of a paper, "The minister was congratulated on being able to get his parish plastered."

"As for any broken answering machine, it goes without saying," puns Wade Boggs, leading hitter for the Boston Red Sox baseball club.

My sister-in-law, Esther Moger, a famed horticulturist, reads a magazine called *Weeders' Digest*.

From sports-buff pundit, Maria Carayas, femme veep at SFM Media Services—
"Do you know Yogi Berra?" Answer: "I'm sorry, I didn't catch that name."
"Do you know Chopin?" Answer: "Yes, we have an old score to settle."
"Did you know J. Edgar Hoover?" Answer: "Gee, man, I didn't."
"Did you know Eli Whitney?" Answer: "Yes, but I didn't cotton to him."
"Did you know Sir Edmund Hillary?" Answer: "I knew him at his peak."

It's no longer the principle of the thing, it's the

interest.

A timid lion tamer kept looking for a protection claws in his contract.

A nuclear physicist is reported to have too many ions in the fire.

Many dishonest merchants become avid sailors. They know how to rig a sale.

"Adam and Eve were thrown out of the Garden because they were too noisy—they raised Cain," puns Jen Damon.

"Popular paperback books always come from the trite side of the racks," puns eye doctor Eliot Finkelstein.

"When I was asked to use 'conscience stricken' in a sentence, I said 'Don't conscience stricken before they've hatched,'" puns jeweler Jim Sullivan of Boston.

"An empty purse is always the same because there is never any change in it," muses Col. Donald M. deHart of Hingham, Massachusetts.

"Sunbathing is a fry in the ointment," puns banker Don deHart II.

"College bred is a four-year loaf out of the old man's dough," notes punster-pharmacist Willie Schwartz of Newton.

More Moaners and Groaners

Bruce Marston of WNEV-TV in Boston says, "What this world needs is a taller hog for people to live higher off!"

Lucy Salhany of Paramount Pictures-TV Distribution puns, "The people who fall asleep at corporate board of directors meetings are bored members, of course."

The Mayor of Boston, Ray Flynn, notes, "A construction worker trying to lose weight should eat his lunch out by the street to curb his appetite."

Barry Thruston of Columbia Pictures-TV tells of a friend of his who worked for a tennis ball manufacturer for six months before getting canned.

Gov. Wallace G. Wilkinson of Kentucky takes time out to puntificate that he saw a sign in a downtown Frankfort shoe store that read "Come in and have a fit."

Carl Woodward, director of marketing at Hunt-Wesson Corporation, punders, "An early TV automobile commercial showed the car itself singing. It was the first car-tune commercial."

James Blumberg, of the same company, adds, "The trouble with getting older is that you discover that nothing recedes like success."

George Becker, president of Sea World, puns, "It should be easy for the Senate to turn over a new leaf. It has plenty of pages."

Why did the brilliant scientist disconnect his door-bell?

He wanted to win the Nobel Prize.

A Barrel of Puns

by William Safire, Esq.,
The New York Times

An epidemic of paronomasia has raced around the world. No longer can the obsession to make puns be xenofobbed off with "paronomasia for the paronomasiatics," the entire English-speaking world is affected.

"The Pun Never Sets On Britain's Empire" was the headline on a dispatch from London by Alan L. Otten of the *Wall Street Journal*. He reported a rash of puns in the British Press.

In the *Observer*, a travel piece about staying in a private home on the island of Crete was labeled "Off

The Cretan Path," a news story about film stars running for Parliament in India was headed "Film Stars Want to Lead Castes Of Millions."

In the *Sunday Telegraph*, a music reviewer panned a performance as "Haydn Seek," prompting listeners to write, asking about "Handel With Care" and "Black Lizst."

The *Guardian* was not to be outpunned. "Distillery Deal Scotched" was one wry headline, and a story about an economic upturn from Tirana, capital of Albania, was headed "Tirana Boom Today."

Here in the colonies, the grand tradition of puntiglio—the Italian word for "word-play," source for our "pun"—is growing apace. The root of this pace-growing is often a headline-writer's need for quick catchiness and has resulted in a new tolerance for a long-despised form of humor. (Am I getting hyphen-happy?) As a certified pundit, I have been obliged to collect specimens over the years.

The Washington *Post* is well hooked pun-wise from its Style section's "Lettuce Now Pick Garden Salads" to a front-page headline over a story on the inception of President Carter's short-lived "New Foundation" theme, "Birth Of A Notion." A transcendental "T" was pronounced in "Hatha Yoga Is Better Than None," and a piece on the Aswan Dam's threatened inundation of the Temple of Dendur was nicely double-punned: "Not By A Dam Site."

The *New York Times Book Review* topped the British "Haydn Seek" with its title to a review about Schubert's songs, "Follow The Lieder." On literary puns, the name of a cocktail lounge in Tucson, Arizona, comes to mind ("Tequila Mockingbirg"). A *Times* feature about an electric car was titled "Nuts And Volts," and a piece on psychiatrist Erik Erickson's fears that civilization was threatened by repression of the urge to have children was headed "Oedipus Wrecks." An Op-Ed piece by the strategist Stanley Hoffman appeared under "New Whine In Old Bottles." And an essay by flamenco guitarist Brook Zern on Spaniards reacting to an American playing their national instrument appeared with this head: "Strum and Drang."

The (New York) *Daily News* covering a potential challenge to Ayatollah Khomeini by Ayatollah Taleghan slugged it "One Ayatollah Too Meini"; along those lines the congressional aide, William Gavin, called a confrontation between the leaders of Iran and the United States "Khomeini Grits."

The Washington *Star* editorially denounced "Catching Tuna Without Porpoise," while a letter writer objected to "too many kooks spoiling the broth." The Los Angeles *Herald Examiner's* analysis of the impact of the metric system was labeled "Take Us To Your Liter."

Magazines have a great fascination for clones: *Newsweek's* derogation of television's second season was "Send In The Clones," and the *New Republic* reached back to Garbo for "I Vant To Be A Clone." A piece in *Harper's* (now defunct) on the difficulty environmentalists were having on the insect issue was titled "Of Mites And Men."

Individuals are happily afflicted with paronomasia, too. Vic Gold, a writer with an instinct for jocularity, offered "Have Gun, Will Cavil," former Representative

A Barrel of Puns

James Symington praised Arthur Burns's "fiscal fitness."
Marshall Bernstein of Roslyn, New York, came up with
a slogan to those opposed to zero population growth—
"Fecund to None." Emil Greenberg of Brooklyn sug-
gested that a porn purveyor be called "a merchant of
Venus" and that the people at Virginia Slims cigarettes
send a message to all test-tube tots, "You've Come the
Wrong Way, Baby!"

The advertising world, print division, is not averse to
puns: a public-service ad for the New York Public
Library said "Read Between the Lions," and an innova-
tive hairdresser in Washington called his relaxing establishment "the most enervative salon in Georgetown."

Poets traditionally play on words. "When I am dead,
I hope it may be said: 'His sins were scarlet, but his
books were read.'" That was Hillaire Belloc long ago.
Recently the poet Peter Viereck made a cushion shot off
Samuel Taylor Coleridge with "ancestral voices pro-
phesying Waugh." That's inside stuff, similar to Vladi-
mir Nabokov's double play in *Pale Fire:* A Curio, "Red
Sox Beat Yanks, 5–4, on Chapman's Homer."

My brother columnist, James J. Kilpatrick, only a
few years ago denounced the revised provisions of the
elections laws as "a case of hashes to hashes, and crust
to crust." I have always been what *Newsweek* called a
"punder on the right." My analysis of the New Arab
wealth was called a "farewell to alms," and a criticism
of an early move toward China was "Peking Too Soon."
I have denounced trendy alienation as "anomie-
tooism," warned of "future schlock," and in Schaden-
freudianship, hailed "urbane renewal." I am ashamed
of knocking the president's drug advisor with "What Is

Past Is Quaalude," and proud of calling supporters of Jack Kemp's tax-cut plan, "Kemp's Followers." The Saudi oil minister's ultimatum was sloganeered in these pages as "Yamani or Ya Life," and only an alert copyreader prevented the first name of the leader of the PLO from being followed by "that's my baby."

Once in a while, puns become part of the language; the "funny bone" is a play on "humerus," the bone that extends from shoulder to elbow. Indulge yourself in this worldwide word-play. There is no more chance of stamping out paronomasia than there is the likelihood of finding a cure to the common cold.

Still More Puns

A radio announcer at KNX was trying to plug a baker's slogan "The Best in Bread." What he actually advised his listeners to get was "The Brest in Bed."

Fred Hooey, a sports announcer on WNAC-Radio, Boston, made radio history during a World Series game when he ad-libbed, "Good afternoon, Fred Hooey, this is ladies and gentlemen." (It ended an illustrious career!)

Keyes Perrin on station WMAS in Worcester, Massachusetts—"The Duck and Doochess of Windsor."

Fred Knight on WOR, New York, "The RAF dropped two- and four-ton blondes on Berlin," and "The weather report—tomorrow rowdy, followed by clain."

Frank Avruche, of Channel 5, WCVB-TV, said, "I can guarantee you to lose weight with my Chinese Diet. You can eat anything—anytime—but you have to use only one chopstick."

Boston *Herald* columnist and Channel 56, WSBK-TV, commentator Howie Carr observed that many politicians begin by wearing vertical pinstriped suits and eventually come out wearing pinstriped suits, but the stripes are horizontal.

I have two ducks that I use as an alarm clock. They wake me up at the quack of dawn.

Two Dutch boys and their mother were standing on the dike looking at the rough sea when suddenly the mother slipped, fell into the ocean, and disappeared. One boy turned to the other and said, "Look, Hans, no mom."

Chronology of sexual activity—triweekly, try weekly, try weakly.

A length of rope went into a bar, sat on a stool, and ordered a beer.
The bartender said, "We don't serve ropes here."
Dismayed and disappointed, the rope went out and then got an idea. He stopped a man and asked, "Will

you please tie a knot in me and separate my strands at both ends?"

This done, he went back into the bar and again ordered a beer.

Said the bartender, "Say, aren't you the same rope who was in here before?"

"No," was the reply, "I'm a frayed knot."

Social diseases—germs of endearment.

Panhandler to a stranger: "I haven't eaten in seven days.

Stranger: "So?"

Panhandler: "That makes one weak, you know."

If Mississippi gave Missouri a New Jersey, what would Delaware? Idaho, Alaska.

In the city of Moscow, there lived a communist named Rudolph. One day the weather suddenly turned terrible.

"Goodness," exclaimed his wife, "snow."

"No," said Rudolph, "it's rain!"

"I still say it's snow," she said.

"Look," he insisted, "Rudolph the Red knows rain, dear.

What do you get if you cross a galaxy and a toad?
Star Warts.

In the early days of Harry Truman's administration, when things were not going too well for him, came the classic line, "To err is Truman."

I had a pet canary
It used to sing so sweet
It flew into the 'lectric fan
Tsk, Tsk . . . shredded tweet!

Did you hear about the overloaded freight train that bit off more than it could choo choo?

What's the funniest animal in the world?
A stand-up chameleon.

If two wrongs don't make a right, what do two rights make?
The first airplane.

While trying to get up from my hospital bed, I asked the attendant to "give me a hand." He responded by applauding. "What are you doing?" I asked. "You asked for a hand," he responded, still clapping. "Here it is."

Mickey Rooney tells about the time he went to a Southern college to gain height. The short actor-comedian said, "They put me on a rack and tied my ankles and neck. Then they stretched the rack."
"Did you gain any height?" I asked.
"No," replied Mickey, "but I confessed to three murders."

Comedian Danny Thomas puns, "In today's modern times, the last thing a woman does by hand is put her finger in a wedding ring."

PUN SONG TITLES

"Since I Put a Bar in the Back of My Car, I've Been Driving Myself to Drink"
"We Were All Out of Firewood, So Father Came Home With a Load"

PUN BOOK TITLE

Life in the Pickle Factory Is Down by the Old Dill Stream

She was only the trainman's daughter—loco with no motive.

She was only the baker's daughter, but she knew what to do with her dough.

George Gobel, the comedian, noted, "It's just as easy to get drunk on water—as it is on land."

A sign in a local dentist's office—
Twice every year your dentist you should see!
Because if you don't, in pain you will be.
When it's time to brush,
Don't get in a rush.
Be true to thy teeth, and they won't be false to thee!

A company in South Africa was giving away firewood. The sign said it was free for the axing!

79

Gene Shalit, the film critic, said of a movie director, "He's given us so many turkeys, he should be made an honorary Pilgrim."

What do ghouls have for breakfast? Scream of Wheat!

What does Dracula take when he has a cold? Coffin syrup.

Faith Thomas defines flying as "faith, hope, and gravity."

"He who hesitates is bossed," quips Anita Meyers.

Peggy Charren of Action for Children's Television Programs puns, "Minds are like TV sets. When they go blank, it is best to turn off the sound."

Old quarterbacks never retire, they just pass away.

On one of the coldest days in Chicago's history, the *Sun-Times* ran a column headed "Have An Ice Day."

AND FROM THE WORLD OF SPORTS

We all know hockey is a fast, dangerous game. Fights break out, penalties are assigned, and the psychological wear and tear on the players is often forgotten because of the physical danger. Many players can't handle the pressures.

One player just couldn't control his temper on the

ice. He would get into fights continually and spend a lot of time in the penalty box. This aggressive behavior is looked on as good, but only up to a point. When you start costing your team wins because you're always in the penalty box, the fans start to get upset. And so it happened. This young player began to get booed unmercifully. He played even more aggressively, but got into more fights and spent more time in the penalty box. Finally, his play was so erratic and time spent penalized so great that the fans started throwing things at him and then even took to spitting on him.

This was too much. The player went to see a psychiatrist. He tried to cope with the booing, and he did, but he couldn't cope with the spitting. The psychiatrist finally told him to retire because he "couldn't solve the spittle of the rinks."

"An overweight male jogger was able to catch up to an attractive female runner long enough to say, 'My pace or yours?' " puns Gary Montanus.

Professional bowlers enjoy their sport. They always seem to have a ball.

Phil Harper, a banker in Waban, notes, "A successful land developer has to have 'plot luck.' "

"Give a woman an inch, and she thinks she's a ruler," notes Linda Crystal of Dow, Jones.

Pardon the Pun

by P. W. Buffington, Ph.D.

Shakespeare, Aristotle, and Swift all agreed—
paronomasia is a whole lot of pun!

It appears that the United States is experiencing an
epidemic of paronomasia. The symptoms include verbal
spontaneity, inflammation of the "humorous" (funny
bone), and much groaning (from the listeners). In
short, the pun is alive and well, even though there are
those who believe that the pun is the lowest form of
"humus."

Paronomasiacs (punsters) have been victimized

throughout history as the pun fell in and out of repute. In psychological defense of punsters, if you enjoy quips, quiddities, and quotes, if your idea of fun is a pun, and if your concept of friendship is a "pun pal," you're in good company.

For instance, Aristotle took time to categorize puns, and Cicero talked up the idea that all great oratories must include a play on words. Not only are puns found in Greek tragedies, but researchers claim the pun's presence in the *Pentateuch* (probably wholly Moses's).

The pun virtually vanished until the sixteenth, seventeenth, and eighteenth centuries when King James I restored the pun to its place of prominence. As a result, Shakespeare played the king's clichés and conundrums, integrating them throughout his works. This finding dates back to 1887. [EDITOR'S NOTE: More on that later.] If Shakespeare's puns were computed today, the number might be slightly inflated.

Other famous punsters include Jonathan Swift and Dr. Samuel Johnson. In fact, Swift's *The Art of Punning* (1719) offered seventy-nine rules that described the nuances of acceptable and unacceptable wordplay.

. . . Many people confuse "spoonerism," double entendres, and Freudian slips. To explain, there is a distinct difference between the pun and the spoonerism, as all dyslexics and dyslogics will attest. The pun is deliberate, the "spooner" accidental. The latter, of course, is named for Oxford's Rev. W. A. Spooner, who was overheard asking in church, "Madam, is this pie occupewed?" Or as the theater usher put it, "Let me sew you to your sheet."

As the purist will tell you, there is also a substantial

difference between the double entendre and the pun. The double entendre is also a word or phrase with two meanings, but one of them usually has a risqué or indecorous connotation. The pun is usually just clean fun.

Finally, Freudian slips are not puns. The difference here, as with the "spooner," is the intention. Freudian slips, technically known as parapraxes, not only relate to "slips of the tongue and pen," but also to mislaying of objects and accidental self-injury. The Freudian slip allows the truth to surface when you didn't consciously want it to emerge.

There truly is a love-hate relationship with puns. You love them if you create them—and hate it if someone beats you to the punch. It's like, "I wish I said that." So, what do you do when you hear a pun? Groan. Although it's music to the punster's ears, that simple groan is a pseudo-putdown. The groan protects you, because you just found yourself one-upped by the guy with the superior vocabulary, and indirectly informs him that you won't put up with his showing off. To say the very least, knowledge of language is a prerequisite to effective punning.

To this writer's knowledge, there are few (if any) empirical studies that test the relationship between punning and intelligence. However, all intelligence-test statistics agree that vocabulary facility and IQ are highly related. Puns are separated from general vocabulary by the former's creativity. In short, to be punny is to be creative.

This creativity exemplifies what psychologists call divergent thinking. To explain, most people use convergent thinking which is narrow and is limited to present facts. Divergent thinking, on the other hand, involves free and fluent mental association, leads the mind to run an almost limitless course, and generates mental comparisons.

Assuming puns to be a form of creativity, the punster is likely to be more flexible and original than the non-punster. Punsters tend to be independent, playful, and nonconformist. Finally, it has been speculated that since creativity allows one to express emotions freely, they may also be less-inhibited people.

The continuum of responses to a pun range from sonorous grunts to hearty guffaws. Somewhere in-between is nervous laughter. Upon hearing a pun (or joke, for that matter), it is the listener's responsibility to respond in order to avoid appearing dense. Nervous laughter usually signals uncertainty. A giggle, plus eyes darting from side to side, may be equivalent to admission that "I don't get it." It may be better to groan or to laugh (gauge from the general behavior of the group) and ask a confidant later to explain.

To close, most people are familiar with single and double puns, but one will occasionally see a triple pun. One example is the boardinghouse made famous by road signs and other media, the Dew Drop Inn. This author is unable to locate a quadruple pun.

Puns are definitely a form of creative verbal expression and are guaranteed to send attention your way. The strokes may be painful if the pun is a "nudger" or near-pun that has to be explained. As every "pun buff" is aware, the moral of the story is (1) o'pun with care, and (2) when in doubt, punt.

A Publisher's Letter

Jesse Birnbaum wants to write a book. It's about celebrities who have been caught unzippered in public.
He's got his title, *Lore of the Flies*. Now all he needs is
a hundred or so anecdotes. And if a theological dispute
breaks out in Egypt, he's got the headline—"Copts And
Rabbis."

Birnbaum, sixty-four, assistant managing editor at
People since 1983, loves the language. He plays it the
way Horowitz plays the piano and Brooks Robinson
played third base (or was that third bass?). Here's his
headline for our recent story about an inn that provides
room cats for its guests—"No Kitten, If You're Feline
Low And Hanker For a Purrsonal Touch, John Hall's
Hotel Is The Cat's Meow." Okay, it's littered wit kitty,
but you've got admire a guy who Cerfs up a headline

with so many puns.

His reputation as a punster was such that Time Inc.'s Editor-in-Chief Henry A. Grunwald, in announcing Birnbaum's appointment to *People,* said it was made "on the condition that he commit no more than two puns in print per week." (At two puns per week, Birnbaum has used up his quota well into the twenty-first century.)

Jess was born in Passaic, New Jersey, one of eight children of a window washer and a housewife. A graduate of Florida Southern College and a veteran of the United States Army Air Force in World War II, he was hired in 1951 as a fill-in music critic at *Time.* His career has since taken him to writing and reporting assignments in San Francisco, London, and Paris, where he was editor of *Time's* European edition. Through it all, there have been the *mots,* each one *mal*-er than the last. In a music review, Birnbaum noted, "It takes an awful lot of brass to play the tuba." The two inevitable burdens of living in New York City are "debt and taxies." The current full-skirt styles for women "cover a multitude of shins." And he replied to a surgeon who wanted to sew up a wound, "Suture yourself."

But Birnbaum isn't all pun and games. As the late-night editor, he often works until 6 A.M. rewriting headlines and overseeing late-breaking stories. He also likes to help writers, both one-on-one and through *Logo File,* his in-house publication that gently tweaks the erring staffer. "My mission in life," he declares, "is to rid the language of clichés, and I am determined to achieve it, come hell or high water."

A *Publisher's Letter*

Donald M. Elliman, Jr.
Publisher
People Weekly

The PUN-ch Bowl

On a road service vehicle—"Call us at any hour. We're always on our tows."

On an electric company truck—"Let us remove your shorts."

Scrawled across a high school wall—"Fite Illiteracy."

A Boston beauty salon calls itself Curl Harbor.

There are nine psychiatrists on my street, which neighbors have nicknamed Psycho Path.

If two is company and three's a crowd, what's four and five?

Nine, what else?

Indecision is the key to flexibility.

A local obstetrician has a sign "Pay as you grow."

There are really only two things you have to worry about in life. One, that things will never get back to normal, and two, that they already have.

Above a wash basin in my office, the boss, Col. Sam Dame, put a large "Think!" sign. Directly below, someone hung a small hand-lettered sign reading "Thoap!"

Did you hear about the cross-eyed teacher they fired last week? She couldn't control her pupils.

Inscription on a flyswatter at Connelly's Hardware Store, in Brookline, reads, "The hand is quicker than the eye is, but somewhat slower than the fly is."

Support your local rescue squad. Get lost.

Posted on an office of a United States air base—"Do Not Undertake Vast Projects with Half-Vast Ideas."

Meatman Milton Shafran of Brookline notes, "The product hospitals recommend you use most is money."

There's no question as to which nation conquers all—determination.

The PUN-ch Bowl

A biology student swallowed a frog this morning and was rushed to the hospital. His teacher expected him to croak at any minute.

A garbage truck had a sign "Always at your disposal."

A lady, rushing outside with her hair in curlers and dressed in an old, raggedy housecoat, called, "Am I too late for the garbage?"

"No," the trashman answered. "Hop right in."

Don't feel bad when you can't clear out your "In" box by the weekend. Only Robinson Crusoe could have everything done by Friday.

WHAT THIS COUNTRY NEEDS . . .

. . . a safety net for people who jump to conclusions
. . . a transmission that will shift the blame
. . . a good no-scent cigar
. . . a song for unsung heroes

THERE'S NO BUSINESS LIKE SNOW BUSINESS

. . . a snowbound town--an ice burg
. . . icicle—a stiff upper drip
. . . ski jump—soar spot

On a car seen at an Indian reservation—"Custer got 'Siouxed.'"

On a small, foreign-made truck—"0 to 65 MPH in 45 minutes."

Spotting a large flock of geese heading south for the winter, a novice bird watcher was heard to exclaim, "Migratious."

The smallest body of water in the United States is Lake Inferior.

A Greek demolition firm is called Edifice Wrecks.

Exercise and diet are the best ways to fight hazardous waists.

The garbage men's ball was a swill affair.

A lion killed a bull and ate it. Then he was so proud, he roared and roared for so loud and so long he didn't hear the hunter sneak up behind him until it was too late. The hunter shot him dead. The moral of this story is when you're full of bull, keep your mouth shut.

Sign on board at Al's frankfurter stand, "What Foods These Morsels Be."

"A clock is like a river because it won't run long without winding," observes Hy Chmara, Boston's leading engraver, as wife Marcia grins.

If only those Las Vegas and Atlantic City lemmings would remember that money can be lost in more ways than won.

"A Peruvian prince fished a beautiful maiden out of a lake and made her his bride before the Inca was dry," says Joe Fitzgerald, sales manager and veep at WLVI-TV, Channel 56, Boston.

No wonder the new student was scared on his first day. All he heard about was the school spirit.

"Literary tests are fetes worse than death," notes Jeffrey Gore, ace student at Babson College, Wellesley.

Barbara Klempner of Beechwood, Ohio, just sent a letter to a garden magazine and signed it "Your constant weeder."

"Oh, no," the waiter exclaimed when he dropped the Thanksgiving dinner. "This means the fall of Turkey, the ruin of Greece, and the breakup of China."

When I was at Warner Brothers Pictures, a fellow writer on Darryl Zanuck's payroll in Hollywood replied to a rival studio that wanted to hire him, "My heart belongs to Fox, lock, stock, and Darryl."

The dictionary is the only place success can be found before work.

Col. Hank Grant, that *Hollywood Reporter* columnist extraordinaire, writes, "I know a starlet who swallowed a spoon and couldn't stir."

The PUN-ch Bowl

A fortune teller advertised that she had medium prices.

David Town Watson of Portland, Oregon, knows a young friend who refers to his tricycle as a "tot rod."

When at first you don't succeed, remember the last four letters of American.

"A Red Sox pitcher with a sore arm was in the throws of agony," admits Col. Mary Jane Ryan, a Boston Red Sox baseball club PR-person.

Surely you know what liars do after they die? They lie still.

This sentense contains threee errors.

The only thing to grow down as it grows up is a duck.

And staying in the poultry vein, the poor farmer's wife had to continually scold the chickens because they used such fowl language.

Don't ever cross a porcupine with a mole. You'll get a tunnel that leaks.

The limestone had a bit of advice for the geology students. "Don't take me for granite."

A little girl fell into a well, and although she cried

plaintively for help, her brother stood by and did nothing. Finally the next-door neighbor came over and pulled the girl up.

"Why didn't you help her?" the neighbor asked the boy.

"I couldn't," the boy replied. "How could I be her brother and assist her, too?"

A word to the wise—never, never iron a four-leaf clover. You'd only be pressing your luck.

What did the grape say when the elephant stepped on it? Nothing, it just let out a little whine.

Leopards are easy prey for hunters. Wherever they go, they're spotted.

They're building a new Russian restaurant on the moon. Don't get too excited. The food may be okay, but there won't be any atmosphere.

It's easy to milk a cow. Any jerk can do it.

Where does dragon milk come from?
Short-legged cows.

An optometrist was advised against moving to Alaska for fear that he might become an optical Aleutian.

Two friends should never do puzzles together. There's always the danger it might lead to crosswords.

The PUN-ch Bowl

An infant prodigy is a child with highly imaginative parents.

It was a disaster when the pink cruise ship hit the purple tanker. Everyone was marooned.

"Charlie's wife was in real trouble when she put firecrackers into his pancakes. He really blew his stack," puns comedian Norm Crosby.

The poor little boy came to school crying. His pet bird, Juan, he told his teacher, had been killed by a golf gun.
"A golf gun?" the perplexed teacher asked. "What's that?"
"I don't know," the sobbing boy answered, "but it sure made a hole in Juan."

It's a known fact that bowlegged cowboys in the Old West had trouble finding work. Nobody wanted to hire them because they couldn't keep their calves together.

Jerry Dominus of CBS puntificates, "Rabbit is a favorite dish in Paris. They raise them in the hutch back of Notre Dame."

Fred Rappaport of CBS-TV reports that when the FBI arrested the head of a Mafia family, he turned out to be a very proud man and kept refusing to answer their questions. They grilled him all night without success, but finally when morning came, the don broke.

PUN-p and Circumstance

A woman and her husband decided to purchase cemetery plots. "We have invested," she said, "in an underground condominium."

A bank stickup was listed as an "unauthorized withdrawal."

Singer Angelo Picardi of Boston had three hit albums. His fourth didn't quite make it, and he attributed that to a "dislocated disc."

We didn't realize how status-conscious people have

PUN-p and Circumstance

become until our newspaper delivery boy insisted we call him a "media courier."

A soldier hid inside a cannon to avoid guard duty, but he was finally discharged.

While working for a personnel agency, my granddaughter, Kathy Bernheimer, of Wesleyan University, Middletown, Connecticut, frequently reviewed application forms. In the blank marked "Position desired," one applicant wrote, "Sitting."

PUN-twisters

Scholarly debate—feud for thought
Four-letter word—par for the coarse
Chronic complainer—the world according to carp

According to my dictionary, "A pun is the humorous use of a word in such a manner as to bring out different meanings or applications, or words alike or nearly alike in sound but different in meaning; a play on words."

Change a key word or two in a familiar saying, and you have a "malaproverb." Here are some choice samples by Mary Y. and Harry W. Hazard as appearing in *Word Ways*.

* Footsore and fancy free.
* A rolling pin gathers no moss.
* Let sleeping bags lie.
* Don't look a sawhorse in the mouth.
* Half a wit is better than none.

* Fools fall in where angels fear to tread.
* Don't kill the goose that laid the deviled egg.
* Don't burn your bridges on both ends.
* Into each cellar some rain must fall.

A man's house is his hassle.

It's better to have loved a short girl than never to have loved a tall.

"Dieting—the triumph of mind over platter," puns pun-pal George Moynihan of the Westinghouse executive staff.

Have you ever wondered if ghosts have Halloween parties? Of course they do. They're always dying to get together.

The cookie was crying because his mother had been a wafer so long.

Recently I was interviewed via radio by a commentator from Melbourne, Australia, which was celebrating a "Pun Week." After a few exchanges of puns, the commentator asked me, "Do you mind if I tell you my favorite pun?"

Since the call was being paid for by the caller, all the way from Melbourne, Australia, I was kind enough to play his straight man. I replied, "What is your favorite pun?"

The Australian began, "What do you call a cow who eats the grass on your front lawn?"

"I don't know," I replied. "What do you call a cow who eats the grass on your front lawn?"

Without hesitation, the Australian said, "A lawnmooer."

This had to be the biggest groaner of the season—Pun Week or no!

Which reminds me, the best-selling soft drink in Australia is Coca-Koala.

Meditation—inner calm system
Ego trip—stumbling over your own feet
Tears—remote code
Sarcasm—barbed ire
Neurotic—a self-taut person
Apathy—vigor mortis
Temper tantrum—call of the riled

ALL IN THE NAME OF SCIENCE

We're all overworked, but a scientist recently came up with a unique solution to his problem. He developed an exact duplicate of himself to help do his work. He labored for two weeks developing a robot that looked, worked, and, in short, was an exact replication of himself. The robot had one flaw. It had the foulest mouth the scientist had ever heard. Try as he might, he couldn't fix the flaw, but the robot did so much work that the scientist got much more done than ever before, and he tolerated the robot's foul mouth.

Of course, the robot's cursing finally became too much, and the scientist decided to get rid of it. One night he packed the robot into the trunk of his car, planning to throw it off a cliff. He drove up the mountain, and when he was certain nobody was looking, he took the screaming, cursing robot from the car and tossed it over the cliff.

Unfortunately, he was seen by two policemen driving by. They stopped him and were about to arrest him when the scientist said, "No, you can't do that. I didn't murder anybody. That was not a human. It was a robot, an exact duplicate of me, and I had to kill it because it cursed incessantly."

The policemen were sympathetic, but they said, "We'll still have to arrest you for making an obscene clone fall."

Ms. Marjorie W. Longley of the *New York Times* quips, "A kiss is the shortest distance between two."

"To keep friends on your side, always offer your candied opinion," says Murray Baker, Boston.

If you run into hard luck while gambling, abandon chip!

My doctor told me I had to have surgery.
"Do I need a second opinion?" I asked.
"Well, you're ugly, too," he replied.

A STORY FROM THE CIA

When the CIA was heavily recruiting espionage agents to combat our intelligence disadvantage during the cold war, two candidates seemed especially promising. They were a sister-brother team. The problem with Wayne and Amber, unfortunately, was that they were always arguing loudly and bickering with each other.

Nevertheless, the CIA was impressed with their loyalty and patriotism, and they passed through the CIA's rigorous training with the highest marks in their class—all the while bickering and screaming at each other. It seemed neither thought the other could do anything right.

Their first assignment was to infiltrate a group of Russian spies who were using restaurants in Paris as fronts for their meetings. Wayne and Amber had, as their assignment, to become familiar with the patrons and goings-on at the various French bistros.

One night they had to visit five different restaurants in an attempt to locate exactly where some Russian activities were taking place. Of course, to protect their covers, they had to behave like patrons of the restaurants—that meant eating and drinking as only the French can.

In order to create the realism they desired, they went from restaurant to restaurant, eating full meals at each and drinking the fine French wines and brandies. They ate like Frenchmen, observed what they could, but, as was their style, continued to argue and shout at each other throughout the meals.

Because this was their first assignment, they were observed by a couple of old CIA veterans. The observers marveled at their vociferous appetites as much as at their constant arguing.

At one point, one observer turned to the other and said, "They're dutiful, voracious spies, but Amber raves at Wayne."

Wanda Ashford, secretary to surgeon Dr. R. Clement Darling, points out that "Alchemists were people who sought a cure for the common gold."

Which burns longer, red candles or blue ones?
Neither, they both burn shorter.

There was never any question who mowed the grass on Walton's Mountain. That was Lawn Boy's job.

Los Angeles Dodgers manager Tommy Lasorda might not agree, but there is a lot of similarity between baseball and pancakes. They both depend on the batter.

Then there was the fellow who made a million dollars from a flea circus by starting from scratch.

At his divorce proceedings, the sculptor's soon-to-be-ex-wife testified, "My husband works in the basement. He's a lowdown chiseler."

Whenever a ghost gets lost in a fog, he's mist.

When she was young, none of skater Sonja Henie's friends laughed when she fell while practicing, but the ice made some awful cracks.

Avid reader Whitney Harris of St. Louis, Missouri,

punned to his wife, Jane, "It may be incorrect to say a book was writ or a book was wrote, but it might be perfectly all right to say a book was wrotten." (Not this one, I hope, Whit.)

Two wrongs don't make a right, but three will get you back on the freeway.—Kiplinger magazine *Changing Times*

Blessed are those who hunger and thirst for they are sticking to their diets.

"The shortest distance between two points depends on who is giving directions," notes David LaCamera of Lordly and Dame, Boston.

"A father was heard describing his teen-ager as surly to bed and surly to rise," comments Col. Dick Sinnott, noted newspaper columnist and radio broadcaster.

Vincent Price made a lot of money working in horror movies. In his case, the end justified the monsters.

An editor at a national magazine calls himself "the fiddler on the proof."

Hypnotist: Imagine you are an Indian teepee. Now imagine you are a wigwam.
Patient: Aw, come on, doc, you're making me two tense. (Two tents.)

The firefly who flew into the fan was absolutely

delighted.

The earth is nothing more than a big bulge that revolves on its taxes.

Fran La Maina, president of Dick Clark Productions puns, "A fief is a robber with a speech defect."

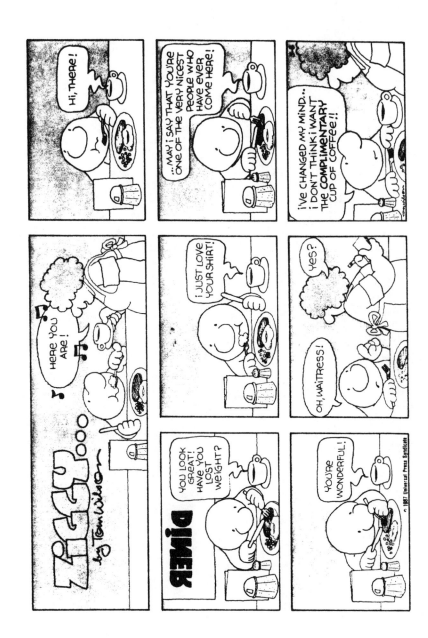

PUN-dit's Corner

SIGNS OF THE TIMES

At a reducing salon—"Twenty-Four Shaping Days Till Christmas"

In front of a beverage store—"Stop Here for Your Holiday Spirits"

On a jewelry shop—"Ring Your Christmas Bell"

On an animal shelter—"Meowy Christmas and Yappy New Year"

At a community college—"If Your Mind Isn't Becoming You, You Should Be Coming Here"

MORE PUN-PER STICKERS

On a Land Rover—"Arf"

Elevator Operator—"Up 234"
Choir Director—"Hmmm"
Driver-Trainer Car—"Beware!"
Postmaster—"Use Zip"

BUSINESS PUN CARDS

Locksmith—"Let me help you out—or in."
Music store salesman—"Come in, pick out a drum, then beat it."
Sleep-shop salesman—"Have water mattress with springs."

"They say TV is still in its infancy, which helps explain why you have to get up and change it so often," says Col. Walter Staab, president of SFM Media Services, New York City.

My wife allows no eating in the living room. She's sort of a one-woman food and rug administrator.

Remarked a customer in the post office, "I'm sending this package by partial post."

A synonym is a word you use in place of one you can't spell.

Overheard at a food store, "Listen, mister, don't upset my apricot."

Quotes Norton Mockridge, "It was just a fig leaf of my imagination."

It's a little known fact that many lighthouse keepers raise hens. Apparently, they like to have their eggs with their beacon.

Boston University's trustee, and my classmate, Nick Apalakis of Stoneham, Massachusetts, comments, "A fellow Greek tore his suit and took it to a tailor named Acropolos from Athens. Mr. Acropolos examined the suit and asked, 'Euripides?'"
" 'Yes,' replied the learned Greek. 'Eumenides?'"

One of Boston's favorite attorneys is Mark Cantor of Callas, Felopoulos, and Ditelberg, who decided on a boat trip for relaxation. On the second day out, Mark somewhat the worse for *mal de mer*, was leaning over the rail of the boat which was rocking badly, when a fellow lawyer sauntered by.
"Can I do anything for you?" he asked Mark.
"Yes," answered Mark, "overrule the motion."

Commenting on her friend's elopement, my daughter-in-law, Marcia, said, "Ah! She put the heart before the course."

Reality is for those who can't face science fiction.

No matter how bad the prose is, it might be verse.

Bigamist—The greedy guy who gets so far
      From being a monogamist
      As to have spouses five, I'd call
      A matrimonial hogamist.

Comedian Joey Adams overheard this. "I have a great lawyer. I broke a mirror, which means seven years bad luck. He thinks he can get me off with five."

Funster/Punster Col./Dr. S. James Coppersmith, general manager and vice president of WCVB-TV, Channel 5, Boston, contributes his favorite pun. It's about a Babylonian general who was declared a traitor for leading a revolt. He escaped the night before he was to be executed and hid in an old Babylonian ziggurat, or temple, where he expected to find some of his associates.

Not finding them, he began to burn the papers they had left and was immediately recaptured.

The moral—WARNING! The searchin' general has determined that smoking ziggurats may be hazardous to your stealth.

I still like best the pun-per sticker on a car that read "Thank God I am an athiest!"

Then there was the woman who brought home an escalator because she bought anything that was marked "Down."

Chuck Brown of The Stout and Big Men's Shop remarks, "With jeans there's no problem finding the right pair—one thighs hurts all."

DAFFY PUNS

Ambition—goaled rush

Awe—wow of silence
Selfishness—a state of mine
Ambivalence—two decides to every question

"A noted senator, who likes to filibuster, calls his speeches 'a wordy cause,'" puns Kay McMahon of Bradenton, Florida.

"Modern fashions look as if they were costume made," puns ABC's 'Jake' Keever.

"Good advice to follow—drive right so more people will be left," puns Col. Peggy Keating at National Amusement Corp., Dedham, MA.

One of my favorate double puns is a sign I saw on a nearby automobile service station. "If you don't get at least eighteen miles per gallon on your car, you auto have your hood examined."

"When turning over a new leaf, it's usually a good idea to turn a few of the preceding pages," notes ABC's Fred Pierce.

Before Oliver Wendell Holmes was a writer, he practiced medicine and taught anatomy at Harvard and Dartmouth. As a practitioner, he was not very successful, for people were a bit doubtful about the flippant youth who posted the following sign above his office door—"Small fevers gratefully received."

"A local doctor's overdue bills now bear a sticker

reading 'Long time no fee,' " puns Academy Award producer, Col. Arnold Kopelson.

Adm. Len Barrack and his wife, Col. Marge Roedig-
Barrack, were discussing an actor they knew. "He's a
nice guy," said Len, "but have you noticed, dear, how
he always lets his friends pick up the dinner check?"

"Yes," replied the beauteous, pert manager of the
Shubert Theater in Boston, "he has a terrible impedi-
ment in his reach."

To make your dreams come true, stay awake.

"Nightclubs are places where the tables are reserved
and the guests are not," observes veteran showman
Julian Rifkin.

Once I thought I was wrong, but I was mistaken.

"Man is the only animal who can be skinned more
than once," says stockbroker Vin Musto of Josephthal
and Company.

"There are three kinds of lies: lies, damned lies, and
statistics," notes accountant Gerry Eidelman of Boston.

"The thing that keeps men broke is not the wolf at
the door, but the silver fox in the window," noted
Capt. Bob Cottle of TV fame.

"A pretty girl who was continually being kissed on
the forehead must have invented high heels," muses

comedian Joey Adams.

"You can call a doctor a quack, but you still can't duck the bill," opines Col. Walter Staab of SFM Entertainment.

Cross poison ivy and a four-leaf clover, and you'll get a rash of good luck.

And don't forget about crossing an earthquake and a forest fire to get shake and bake.

PUN-ography and Other Gems

This is my favorite double-barreled pun.

An American tourist went to France and visited the famous Notre Dame Cathedral. Approaching the Quasimodo-like caretaker, he said, "I've traveled all this way from the United States to hear the famous cathedral chimes ring. Can you oblige me, please?"

The caretaker said, "Unfortunately, the bell is broken. It has no clapper inside. The only way you can hear it ring is to pull this rope, and when the bell starts to sway, put your head inside the bell. Your head will serve as the clapper."

So the tourist did as he was told. He tugged on the bell's rope very hard, and the bell began to sway back and forth with great speed. The tourist put his head inside the bell as it came by with a mad rush. The force of the swinging bell pushed him over the railing, and he fell to his death, four stories below.

A crowd gathered to witness the demise of the tourist, who lay splattered on the pavement. A gendarme approached the caretaker, who stood nearby, and asked, "Do you know who this man is?"

The caretaker replied, "No, but his face rings a bell."

A few years later, the victim's twin brother visited the same Notre Dame Cathedral and approached the same caretaker, asking, "Can I hear the famous Notre Dame Cathedral bell chimes?"

The caretaker said, "The bell is broken. There is no clapper inside. However, if you pull the rope and make the bell swing, then put your head inside when it comes by, you'll be able to hear the chime."

The tourist did as he was told. However, like his twin brother before him, he pulled the rope with too much force. When it came by and he inserted his head into the bell, he, too, was catapulated over the railing and fell to his death four stories below.

As the broken body lay on the pavement, a gendarme asked the caretaker, "Do you know this man, monsieur?"

The caretaker took a quick look and replied, "No, but he's a dead ringer for his brother."

The explorer came down from the North Pole. When he reached the last Lapp, he knew he was at the

Finnish line.

A man bumped into an old friend in New Orleans and punned, "How's bayou?" (That's from lyricist Alfred Sherman of Boston.)

"A man moved into Kansas City with the firm belief that Missouri loves company," puns Col. Bob Parsons of Boston.

A man once took milk of amnesia to forget his problems.

Someone defined a gold digger as a human gimme pig.

In commenting about actress-swimmer Esther Williams, someone punned, "A lot of water has flowed over this dame."

Pat Roedig of Taft Communications puns, "I know a starlet who pointed to her shapely legs and said they are still see-worthy."

Don't you find that the people who think they know everything are always bugging those of us who do?

MORE PUN-Y NEWSPAPERS

In a Chicago *Downtown News* story about airline personnel—"Continental paid tribute to a flighty attendant."

121

From an article on a boxing match in the Roanoke, Virginia, *Times and World News*—"One official voted a draw, and the other two spit on the winner."

Travel ad in the Chicago *Daily News*—"Ski Boyne Country, two-day special includes lifts, lodging, and males."

From the Washington *Post*—"The Metropolitan Edison Company aborted the planned entry of two unclear engineers into the building housing the damaged reactor."

Classified ad in the Laguna Niguel, California, *Oceanside South Pennysaver*—"Cremation Service, Lifetime membership: $25 couple, $15 single."

"I met a fellow who had the Midas touch. Everything he touched turned into a muffler," notes travel-celebrity booker Bernie Garber.

A boy's pet bird fell into a can of varnish and drowned.

"It was a sad way to die," he told his Uncle Rory, "but he sure had a beautiful finish."

This is one of my favorite puns.

Does the name "Red" Adair conjure up a celebrity in your mind? Many years ago, Mr. Adair was known as an expert in putting out oil-well fires, which were prevalent in the Texas oil fields and elsewhere. So widely known was he that a credit card company (he wouldn't leave home without one) publicized him on television nationally. He suddenly became a household byword.

One evening he went to a local bar and said to the

bartender, "I'd like a Scotch and water, please. You know who I am, don't you?"

The bartender looked at Mr. Five-by-five and replied, "No, I don't recognize you. Am I supposed to know who you are?"

Red's ego deflated, and he slowly began to drink his beverage. Just then a drunk walked into the bar, sat beside Adair, and whispered to him, "Aren't you Red Adair?"

Suddenly the robust little Texan became nine feet tall. He couldn't believe that someone would recognize him in this dimly lit bar. He replied, "Yes, I am Red Adair."

To which the drunk replied, "Tell me, are you still [bleeping] Ginger Rogers?"

One recalls the story of Mrs. Nancy Reagan, the first lady, at a state dinner, discussing democracy with a Japanese ambassador.

"And when did you last have an election?" she asked the Oriental dignitary.

"Before blekfast," he replied, with some embarrassment.

Mexican vacationists Alice and Ezra Sherman of Boston saw a recent Mexican weather forecast calling for "Chili today and hot tamale."

Tarzan ran into Jane's tent and shouted, "It's a jungle out there," according to Bob "Perlie" Perlstein, SFM Veep.

123

Headline in the Boston *Herald* recently—"Gillette Survives Second Half By A Close Shave." (Referring to a proposed takeover.)

The Boston *Globe* headlined—"Martin Has A Nose For 'Cyrano.'" (Referring to Steve Martin's film, *Roxanne*, a modern version of the life of Cyrano de Bergerac.)

The Philadelphia *Daily News* had the audacity to run this headline—"Jane [Fonda] To Vets—Sorry I Hanoied You."

The famous husband-wife doctor team of Drs. Eng Hwi Kwa and Sew-Leong of West Newton, Massachusetts, regaled their two children, Kenneth and Jason, with those story of Fu Manchu and his daughter, Cherry Blossom, who were on a tour of New England in the company of a young man.

The trio visited a pair of water slides on a mountainside and took several rides. When the three went down the chute together, Cherry Blossom and her boyfriend were decorous; but when it was just the two of them, they embraced each other passionately.

"Cherry Blossom," the young man said, "I really like it when your father isn't with us, and you hug and kiss me!"

"Yes," she replied, "but I can only do that when the Fu is in the other chute."

CARD GAMES AND PLAYERS

Hearts—cardiologist
Pinochle—a mountain climber
Cribbage—a new parent
Gin rummy—Gene Rummy

The cook was a good cook, as cooks go. And as cooks go, she went.

What is the difference between an angry circus owner and a Roman barber?
One is a raving showman, and the other is a shaving Roman.

Why is life like a shirt button?
Because it only hangs by a thread.

When is an eye not an eye?
When an onion makes it water.

A carpet is bought by the yard and worn by the foot.

A drama critic is a person who leaves no turn unstoned.

PUN-tunes

Opera tryouts—	trial and aria
Classical jazz—	rock of ages
Serenade—	swan song
Yodeling—	slope opera

MORE HEADLINE BOO-BOOS

Over an article in the Milwaukee *Journal* about circus-coming-to-town festivities—"Dalmations Get Choice Spots In Parade."

In the Minneapolis *Star and Tribune*—"Congressman Dips Into Pork Barrel To Bring Home Bacon."

A story in the Des Moines *Register* about highway conditions—"R ads Acr ss 1 Was Ch ck Full Of H les."

On an item in the Montgomery County, Maryland, *Journal*—"Beer Shortage Has Merchants Frothing."

Comedian Henny Youngman admits he was born to be a musician. He has a fiddle in his hands and a bow in his legs.

The acrobat really liked his Christmas presents. In fact, he flipped over them.

Remember the good old days when Uncle Sam lived within his income and without yours?

News commentator Barbara Walters is widely known for her lateral lisp—finding it difficult to pronounce the letters "r" and "l"—which hasn't impaired her success as a television celebrity.

One afternoon she visited a flea market and bought a "genuine" letter signed by the famous Mark Twain. She showed it to a friend with great excitement. The friend looked at the letter and saw only the letter "X" signed at the bottom.

"I see only the letter 'X,'" said her friend. "What does that mean?"

Barbara replied, "Oh, that's his 'Mark.'"
"Where's the 'Twain?'" asked her friend.
"The twain is at the waiwode station," answered Barbara, unabashed.

QUICKIE PUNS

Piano tuner—	"grand"
Waiter—	"tipical"
Author—	"all write"
Flying instructor—	"soaring"
Car dealer—	"it auto increase"

Women discuss their wardrobes chic-to-chic.

COLORFUL PEOPLE

Melon of Troy
James Blond
Imogene Cocoa
Willie Maize

Congressional PUN-dits

In a speech in Congress, Rep. Silvio Conte of Massachusetts gave his views on the "Freedom Peach Research and Education Act."

"This bill may be a plum for peach peddlers, but it is a pit for friends of fuzzy fruits. I cannot swallow it. Anyone who believes that money grows on trees is going to wind up in a jam. Once again, the agriculture committee has taken leaf of its senses. Any member who votes for it deserves a raspberry from voters."

From the *Wall Street Journal*—
Rep. Bob Michel of Illinois was incensed at our

WINSTON
BY BURNETT & SAJEM
I HAVE A GREAT, GREAT UNCLE THAT WAS RUN OVER BY WELLS FARGO
3-14
TELL US ABOUT IT...
HE SUFFERED FROM STAGE FRIGHT THE REST OF HIS LIVES.
PA DUM PUM!
© News America Syndicate, 1987

editorial in which we demoted House Speaker Thomas "Tip" O'Neil from "Czar" to "Czardine." Mr. Michel rose to the Speaker's defense on the House floor. "Czardine?" he mused. "There's something fishy here. Did the *Journal* use the word on porpoise? If so, this is a whale of a story, and there is salmon wrong with it. Unless the *Journal* retracts what it said, its editors will soon be singing a different tuna.

"Trout history such journalism has been deplored. It is bass. As for the Speaker, eel have to defend himself. This strikes to the sole of the House, for too long there have been charges that we flounder. So I say to the Speaker, where there's a gill, there's a way."

The editorial, we understand, gave the Speaker a splitting haddock.

This is probably an apocryphal story, but it also concerns the former House Speaker "Tip" O'Neill, who was asleep when his wife, Millie, nudged him and whispered, "Tip, I think there's a burglar in the house."

Mr. Speaker opened his eyes and said, "A robber in the House? Never! In the Senate maybe!" And promptly went back to sleep.

The Pun Never Sets . . ."

by Alan L. Otten

The article in Britain's *Sunday Observer* told about two young farmers making cheese from sheep's milk. "Farm Put To Good Ewes," read the headline. A transcendental meditation group took over a country estate, *Spectator* magazine noted, and padded the floor and walls of the former billiard room so that the TM-ers could practice levitation there. The caption on the story—"The Landed Gently." A feature in the *Guardian* relayed a Majorca hotelkeeper's complaint about frequent need to repair or replace beds broken by overly energetic honeymooners. The headline—"It's Called Pillow Torque."

American magazines and papers also pun from time to time, but certainly with nothing like the frequency or abandon of the British. Peter Preston, editor of the *Guardian*, one of the punniest of Britain's papers, says his favorite headline dealt with a dispatch from Tirana, the capital of Albania, telling of an economic revival underway there. The headline: "Tirana Boom Today." A *Guardian* feature on a handful of privately owned coal mines—not run by the British government's National Coal Board—was titled "Mining Their Own Business," while a food column with recipes for cooking rabbit was called "Hare Cuts."

The *Observer* is another avid pun-practitioner. A column discussing why so many women tend to fall for priests and religious gurus was headed "Hooked by the Celibate." A travel piece on the pleasures of staying in private homes on the island of Crete was labeled "Off the Cretan Path," while the editor handling a news story about movie stars running for Parliament in India came up with this head: "Film Stars Want to Lead Caste of Millions."

A story in the *Sunday Telegraph* suggesting that British tax men might crack down on company-supplied cars and other management perquisites was headlined "The Revenue's 'No Perking' Signs."

Even the *Sunday Times* succumbs every so often. When the Hunt brothers—Nelson Bunker and William Herbert—testified before a congressional committee on their silver-trading activities, the story was headed "The Silver-Tongued Battle of Bunker on the Hill."

—Alan L. Otten

The Puns
of Shakespeare

by Dr. F. A. Bather, F.R.S.

The original typescript of this paper is in the New City
Public Library. it is based on the author's article in
Noctes Shakespeariance, Winchester College, 1887.

Nearly all the commentators on Shakespeare fell foul
of the puns. Sir Sidney Lee, in his *Life of Shakespeare*,
speaks of the depths of vapidity to which Shakespeare
and contemporary punsters could sink. But it is more
important to understand than to censure. The pun was

a pervading element in Elizabethan literature and an important factor in the method of our early dramatists.

Why did the Elizabethans indulge in the verbal jesting? Some think it childish and that suggests the answer. Children, as they acquire the use of their mother tongue, delight to play with it. They make up jingles and seize on resemblances of sound. They revel in punning riddles, and often some unfortunate name will dissolve a class in laughter. So, too, as nations fashioned for themselves a language, they loved to prove their mastery of it in similar ways. Almost all literatures have passed through a stage in which the pun was an approved figure of speech. There are puns in the *Pentateuch*, in the great dramas of the Greek, in Cicero and Virgil. In Japanese poetry, wordplay and similar artifices are among the most admired ornaments.

The philosophy of the pun would lead us far. It is enough to observe the pleasure we take in an unexpected association of distinct ideas. A pun effects this by a similarity of sound. But it is clear that an association by unifying thought is deeper and truer than an association by the accident of language. Wit can be translated into another language, but if it resides merely in words, it vanishes. The later Roman writers on style recognized this, and verbal jesting disappeared from serious composition. But when Latin ceased to be the only language of literature, when the various languages of Europe came into their own, history repeated itself. The Elizabethans inherited a tongue in which two strains of Norman-French and Anglo-Saxon had at last fused, and during the process had been enriched by contributions from sources so diverse as Scandinavia and ancient Rome. Englishmen discovered what a wonderful instrument their language was, and they delighted to play on it. Later critics again dwelt on how superficial was the humour of the pun, and once more it disappeared from all productions that can claim to be called literary.

The development of the individual repeats in little the development of the race. Just as the pun, for the reasons above mentioned, fell into disuse among dramatists, so may it be expected to show a gradual decline in the works of him, who more than any other, is the representative of those dramatists. That this is largely the case has been recognized in general principle by those who have studied Shakespeare's plays from a chronological standpoint. This the late Professor [Edward] Dowden writes, "Shakespeare's early conceits, puns, frequent classic allusions, occasional overwrought rhetoric, all gradually disappear or subside; but these changes really belong to the growth of Shakespeare's taste and judgment." Still, no one before 1881 had attempted the scientific method of bringing this theory to the bar of fact. On the contrary, all would have said with Dowden, "These are the things that cannot be precisely weighed and measured, although they can be clearly felt." Fleay, for instance, says of this metrical test that in it only can quantitative results be obtained.

When I was a boy in Winchester, it occurred to me that it should be possible to apply the statistical and scientific method to at least one of the points mentioned by Dowden. I, therefore, undertook the complete study of Shakespeare's verbal jests and quibbles. One might think that any person of intelligence should be able to see these things for himself without applying the ponderous method of statistics. Unfortunately, the purely aesthetic criticism depends so greatly on the personality of the critic that its conclusions are often more entertaining than exact.

To Professor Dowden himself, for instance, no one will deny a large measure of aesthetic sense. And yet, hear what he says regarding the contrast of characters in *The Two Gentlemen of Verona*. "The *bright* and clever Sylvia is set over against the tender and ardent Julia; the clown Speed, notable as a *verbal wit* and *quibbler*, is set against the humorous Launce." After noting the words emphasized, you may perhaps be surprised to learn that whereas Julia quibbles eleven times, Sylvia only quibbles once. The contrast may exist, but it does not lie in the quality of wit. As regards Speed and Launce, Dowden has more right on his side, for Speed makes twenty puns, and Launce makes but nineteen. Another aesthetic critic, Mrs. Elizabeth Montagu, in her essay on the writings and genius of Shakespeare (1769), says, "As Falstaff, whom the author certainly intended to be perfectly witty, is less addicted to quibble and play on words than any of his comic characters, I think we may firmly conclude he was sensible. It was but a false kind of wit, which he practiced from the hard necessity of the times."

What are the facts. In *I King Henry IV*, there are forty-seven puns, of those Falstaff makes twenty-one, Prince Hall ten, Hotspur eight. In *II King Henry IV*, there are fifty-two puns. Falstaff leads with twenty-seven, Prince Hal is again a bad second with six. In *The Merry Wives of Windsor*, there are thirty-nine puns, of which eleven are credited to Falstaff, this being twice as many as are made by anyone else in the comedy. No character in the whole of Shakespeare's plays, or in those of any contemporary dramatist with which I am acquainted, exceeds Falstaff in quibbling. Were Sir John alive to read the above-quoted remark of Mrs. Montagu, he would surely once more ejaculate, "Lord, Lord, how the world is given to lying."

In 1881, when I began this study, the chronological order of Shakespeare's plays was not so accurately determined as it has been since. It was, however, generally agreed that Shakespeare's plays could be separated into four main periods which were thought to correspond with events and stages in the author's life. These were regarded as

   (I)   a period of apprenticeship
   (II)   a period of manly vigour
   (III)   a gloom period, and then
   (IV)   a period of final calm.

According to that theory, a gradual decrease of puns was to be expected in succeeding periods. Taking the plays at that time allotted to the respective periods, the following were the proportions (percentages of puns) actually found.

   I) 2.12; II) 1.36; III) .49; IV) .48.

Taking the chronology now generally accepted and dividing the plays into four corresponding periods, I find a rather different set of figures. The first period from 1519–1594 (that is to say from *Love's Labour's Lost* to *King John*), gives a percentage of 1.98. The second period from 1594–1600 (that is to say from *A Midsummer Night's Dream* to *Twelfth Night*) gives 1.25. The third period from 1600 to 1609 (which includes the Roman plays and the great tragedies) yields a percentage of .63; while the last period of romantic tragicomedy, belonging to the years 1610 and 1611, gives .42. These latter numbers if compared with the former, show apparently a more equable decrease in the number of puns. But if we divide the first period in two parts, the first containing *Love's Labour's, The Two Gentlemen of Verona, Comedy of Errors,* and *Romeo and Juliet,* approximately the same plays as were contained in the first period of our former division, then this first half gives the percentage of 2.97, slightly higher than before, but the second half drops to 1.13, which is rather lower than the percentage of the next division. The reason for this will be seen directly. Meanwhile, it is interesting to observe that more accurate knowledge concerning the chronology of Shakespeare's plays, while by no means corroborating the old and somewhat fanciful division, based more largely on purely esthetic criticism, still does agree even better with our main hypothesis that there was a gradual decrease of punning as Shakespeare advanced in his art.

It may be well to pause here to explain how these numbers are calculated. Each play was read with extreme care and every jest that depended on words alone, every double meaning, and every quibble noted. On a first reading, many puns escaped notice, but these were usually detected afterwards by analogous undoubted puns in other plays by Shakespeare or by contemporary authors. For example (Act II, Scene 2, line 271), Hamlet says to Rosenkrantz and Guildenstern, "Shall we to court?" They reply, "We'll wait upon you." Hamlet: "No such matter. I will not sort you with the rest of my servants." Here I was at first doubtful, but on finding a similar passage in Ben Jonson, I am now sure that a quibble was intended.

Silent Woman: I,1, p. 411a:

LaFoole: I am come to entreat you to wait upon two or three ladies to dinner to-day?

Clericourt: How, sir! Wait upon them! Did you ever see me carry dishes?

LaFoole: No, sir. Dispense with me. I meant to bear them company.

The number of puns having been ascertained, the lines were counted in the Globe edition and the number of puns per one hundred lines determined. This reduced all to a common standard. The necessity for this will be made clear by an example: there are forty puns in *Much Ado About Nothing*, thirty-seven in *Comedy of Errors*, but there are only 1,776 lines in the latter play and 2,825 in the former; so that the percentages are— *Comedy of Errors*, 2.08, *Much Ado About Nothing*, 1.42.

When you make a diagram of the plays by the years in which they appeared and apply these percentages, you will end up with a gradually descending curve, the descent being more rapid at the beginning. This, in the main, corroborates our hypothesis. In the exuberance of youth, his brain thick with teeming fancies, his mind impressed with the euphuistic style of the day, Shakespeare simply revelled in his mastery of the language and was no doubt eager to show that whatever others could do, he, at any rate, could go one better. But, with *Romeo and Juliet* once behind him, he discarded the tendency to introduce puns on every possible and impossible occasion, and, for all that the critics may say, in subsequent plays, puns are generally used either appropriately to the character speaking or with some other dramatic effect. This, however, does not prevent a continued decrease of punning, until the lowest point is reached in one of the latest plays, *Cymbeline*. This decrease is correlated with other well-known changes, a greater profundity of thought, a closer and more elliptical style, and a more forcible, less regular metre.

So much for the general curve. When we turn to consider details, especially the apparent aberrances, we find that they yield a ready explanation, perfectly consistent with the general hypothesis.

We first notice the sudden drop in *Richard III*. Here, we have to remember that between *Romeo and Juliet* and *Richard III*, there were produced the various parts of the revised version of *Henry IV*. Not only were they revisions, Shakespeare cooperated with another writer who is generally believed to have been Christopher Marlowe. That poet, as we all know, gained his effect by the splendour and vigour of his words and rarely turned aside to trifle. The percentage of puns in *Henry VI* is, therefore, extremely small. Marlowe was killed in June, 1598, but *Richard III* was undoubtedly written under his influence. The same is the case with *Richard II*. It is, therefore, easy to understand why these plays should be relatively free from puns, but the Euripidean dialogue in *Richard III* and the general inaptness of the puns in *Richard II* are a setoff against their numerical weakness.

Just as Shakespeare's *Richard II* is obviously reminiscent of Marlowe's own *Edward II*, so Shakespeare's *Merchant of Venice* was suggested by and still bears traces of Marlowe's *Jew of Malta*. Nonetheless, Shakespeare was gradually throwing off the influences of Marlowe, and this is seen in the puns no less than in the general treatment so that by the time *King John* is reached, we find the percentage of puns not very far below that of *Romeo and Juliet*.

But here again, there is a sudden drop in *A Midsummer's Night Dream*. For this there seems to be special reasons. The play is very different in character from any other play by Shakespeare. It is more in the style of a masque. It is a poem and written in rhyme for the most part. It was probably composed, as Sir Sidney Lee suggests, to celebrate a marriage in high society. We may go even further and assume that it was actually performed for the first time before the contracting parties. Shakespeare, who knew all too well how to accommodate himself to his surroundings, entertained his courtly audience with airy fancies and delicate poetry rather than with those jests wherewith he had occasionally condescended to tickle the ears of the groundlings.

In *The Taming of the Shrew*, the next play, the case is reversed. Here we have a roaring farce, or, if not entirely that, at least a comedy that has to be played with a strong farcical spirit. So much is this the case that in order to give it the right setting, there is an Introduction and the comedy is further removed from reality by being presented to us as a play within a play.

All's Well That Ends Well furnishes a rather more interesting problem—more interesting because it is rather more difficult. In this play, as Sir Sidney Lee points out, "early and late features of Shakespeare's work are perplexingly combined. The proportion of rhyme to blank verse is high, and the rhymed verse in which epistles are penned by two of the characters (in place of prose) is a clear sign of youthful artifice . . . On the other hand, nearly half of the play is in prose and the metrical irregularities of the blank verse and its elliptical *teneur* are characteristics of the author's ripest efforts." Although Sir Sidney Lee places the comedy in 1595, this is only on the somewhat doubtful evidence of [the critic] Francis Mere's allusion in 1598. Still, he points out that the play is not known in any edition earlier than the First Folio, and the discrepancy of style suggests that the Folio text presents a late revision of an early draft.

In the three plays that followed, it is interesting to observe how the puns gradually increased in quality as Falstaff acquired prominence, and how, with his disappearance, they fell again to a normal level in *Henry V*. The high number found in *The Merry Wives of Windsor* is, of course, due to the fact that this is nothing more than a farce, written, as the story goes, in the space of a fortnight. It seems to have been revised later. Nonetheless, certain passages seem to show that there may have been a part sketched out by the author at an earlier date (namely, the bitter allusions to Sir T. Lucy, his coat of arms, and the deer stealing). The large number of Latin words is also a characteristic of early plays, perhaps while Shakespeare's schooling was still fresh upon him.

Nothing more calls for comment until we come to the three plays *Julius Caesar, Hamlet,* and *Troilus and Cressida.* In *Julius Caesar,* the percentage is low, and in *Hamlet,* it occupies about the position that it would have if the curve were regular, but in *Troilus and Cressida,* it again rises slightly.

The fact is that there is a great deal of difficulty connected with the chronology of these plays. In a previous paper, I treated *Julius Caesar* as one of the doubtful plays, since at that time a view was prevalent that Shakespeare had written it in collaboration with some other writer, possibly Ben Jonson. No mention, however, is made of this view in Sir Sidney Lee's *Life of Shakespeare.* At the same time, as regards the chronology, Sir Sidney says, "Internal evidence alone determines the date of the composition."

The internal evidence on which he relies is the characterization, the metrical features, and the deliberate employment of prose. "All three traits," he says, "suggests a composition of the midpost point of the dramatist's career." It is, however, perfectly legitimate to add to the argument the evidence provided by the puns. This would certainly entitle us to place the play at a somewhat later date.

As regards *Troilus and Cressida* also, Sir Sidney says the difficulties of determining the date are very great. All we know is that in February, 1603, the publisher, James Roberts, obtained a license "for the book of *Troilus and Cressida* as it is acted by my Lord Chamberlain's men"; if the play was acted before this, it must obviously have been written still earlier. And the regularity of blank verse to which Sir Sidney alludes, as contrasted with the greater irregularity of *Julius Caesar*, might even suggest that these two plays should change places in our scheme. If this were done, the descent of the curve would be almost normal. *Hamlet*, which is perhaps the play most characteristic of our author's genius, was written by him at the midmost point of his career, and we find that the pun ratio also occupies about the mean position. It is, no doubt, a little high if *Hamlet* be considered as a tragedy and compared with the great tragedies of the succeeding period.

Hamlet, however, is a singularly composite play. It no doubt retains fragments of its predecessors by less-experienced hands and incorporates in its final form a large amount of topical and purely temporary matter, as for instance, the controversial references to contemporary theatrical history.

Hereafter, the level of the puns drops and remains low all through the period of the late tragedies, only rising again in *The Tempest*. The rise is clearly due not to any emergence from a supposed period of gloom, but to the introduction of a strongly satiric and comic element brought from the outer world as a contrast to the mystical wonders of the remote island.

I would here draw your attention to a point which I have not previously seen noticed. It is the contrast between the rapidity of production in the early years of Shakespeare's career and the relative slowness of its latter half. In reality, the contrast was even greater than it appears because in the first half should also be included Shakespeare's contribution to the three parts of *Henry VI,* the publication of his poems, and a good deal of dramatic hackwork, the tradition of which remains in the ascription to Shakespeare of such plays as *Titus Andronicus, Arden of Feversam,* and *A Yorkshire Tragedy.* It is particularly noticeable how the period of world masterpieces was issued in by a year of comparative rest—and how during the first eight years of the seventeenth century, these were produced at a rate of only one a year. It is clear that Shakespeare pondered more deeply over the subject matter, that he devoted more conscious attention to the style, and that, probably with no less conscious attention, he deliberately rejected the artifice of wordplay except when needed for a forcible dramatic effect.

. . . The pun, despised of the commentators, may seem but a small thing. Yet if any among you be incited to continue the study, he will find it leads to many interesting fields of research. He will learn how the pronunciation of our English tongue has altered the last three centuries, though the Cockney and several other dialects will retain some of the old sounds. He will become acquainted with many a curious custom and the slang terms derived from it. Many a passage that was before dark and perhaps meaningless will have for him meaning and beauty. He may even gain boldness to proceed to conjectural emendation of the text, for a pun in one place is often so closely simulated in another that the change of a letter would elucidate the sentence and make it, as the commentators say, "much more in the author's manner." Finally, he will gain an increased reverence for the man who had such a command over a newly framed language that he could perpetrate in it the large number of ten hundred and sixty-two puns.

F. A. Bather
Wimbledon, England, 1887

PUN-Abridged Dictionary

(From A to Z)

–A–

a.	A letter that is often written but never mailed
abbrev.	The abbreviation of abbreviation
AWOL	Rockie hooky
Academy Awards	A place where everyone lets off esteem

Accident	A condition in which presence of mind is good, but absence of body is better
Accordian	An instrument whose music is long drawn out
Acrobat	The person who turns a flop into a success
Acorn	An oak in a nutshell
Adam's Rib	The original bone of contention
Advertising	15 percent commission and 85 percent confusion
Advertising executive	Yessir, nosir, ulcer
Afternoon snack	The pause that refleshes
Afterdinner speech	The highest possible longitude and the lowest possible platitude
Associate producer	About the only guy in Hollywood who will associate with a producer

–B–

Bachelor	A man who never makes the same mistake once
Bagpipes	The original Scotch high bawl
Band	An orchestra without guts
Barber	The town cutup
Barbershop	A clip joint where you get trimmed by experts
Baseball	A business that can't thrive without strikes

Bon vivant	A man who would rather be a good liver than have one
Borscht	Beet soup with high blood pressure
Boudoir	Room for improvement
Brassiere	A bust stop
Brochure	A handbill with kid gloves

–C–

Camel	An animal that ruined its shape trying to get through the eye of a needle
Cockfighting	Fowl play
Cocktail	A drink to wet the appetite
Columnist	A paragrafter
Comedian	A man with a pun-track mind
Compliment	The applause that refreshes
Contortionist	A man who leads a double life
Convalescent	A patient who is still alive; or a person in bed and bored
College Boy	A young man who likes ties with dots, suits with stripes, and letters with checks
Cranberries	Grapes with hypertension

–D–

Disc jockey	A guy who lives on spins and needles
Divorce	Long division
Dog	The only friend you can buy for money

Dollar sign   An "S" that has been double-crossed

–E–

Easy chair   The hardest one to find empty

Ego   I-dolatry

Egoist   A guy who is always me-deep in conversation

Embezzlement   Bankers away!

Etiquette   The noise you don't make eating soup

–F–

Fire   It makes light of everything

Fish   Brain food because it travels in schools

Flour   A word by any other name would smell as wheat

Freudian ship   A foot-in-mouth disease

Fright   An emotion that starts with a start

Frown   A smile turned upside down

Frump   A woman who looks her age and doesn't try to overlook it

–G–

G   The end of "everything"

Garage   Something usually built with a house attached

Gardener	A man who never lets grass grow under his feet
Garlic	A food never eaten by those who practice breath control
Genius	Unrecognized talent
Gout	Exterior, as "the kid is grown gout of his clothes."
Grandfather	"An OK AK"
Grapefruit	Eyewash
Guillotine	The only sure cure for dandruff

–H–

Hack	A writer who makes a living
Haig & Haig	Two Scotchmen who died many years ago but whose spirits live on
Hair	The only thing that will prevent baldness
Hug	Energy gone to waist
Hush money	The proof that money talks and also stops talk

–I–

Ice	One of the few things that really is what it's cracked up to be
Illegal	A sick bird
Ingenue	An actress who gets billing by cooing

–J–

Jelousy	The friendship one woman has for another
Jigsaws	What the people in Japan ride in
Jittery	N-n-nervous
Joke	A jestnut
Judge	A lawyer who knew a judge; of a law student who marks his own papers

–K–

K	As in "knot" but not in "not"
Kangaroo	An animal who carries her brood in a snood
Kiss	Something that is taken at face value
Kindred	Fear that relatives are coming to stay
Knighthood	Honor bestowed by a king to change the subject
Knockout	A woman who can box

–L–

Lamb	An animal that gets more sheepish with age
Landlord	A man who aims to lease
Laplander	The most awkward man on a crowded bus
Laundry	A business that always has clothes competition
Lawsuit	Generally a loss-suit

Life	A play with a lousy third act
Lifeguard	Beachnut
Lisp	To call a spade a thpade
Lock	A thing that's all keyed up

–M–

Martyr	A self-made hero
Mason-Dixon Line	The boundary between you-all and youse
Mauve	Pink trying to be purple
Mayor	A he-horse
Medicine	A drug on the market
Menu	A list of dishes the restaurant has run out of
Merry-go-round	A vehicle for getting nowhere quickly
Mickey Finn	A liquid blackjack
Middle age	The time a man starts turning out the lights for economical rather than romantic reasons
Middleman	One who works both ends against the middle
Minister	A man who collects the "I do's" for the union
Moon	A sky light
Moron	A person who is more off than on
Mother	Mom's the word
Mother-in-law	A mother in-awe

Mugwump	An animal that sits on a fence with its mug on one side and its wump on the other
Mustard plaster	A bosom friend

–N–

N	A letter in transit
Nationality	A state of being a state
Naught	Something that is nothing
Navel	A useful place for holding salt while one eats celery in bed
Necking	A passion fancy
Nepotism	A form of favoritism—relatively speaking
Net	A lot of little holes tied together with string
Noose	The tie that binds
Numb	A sensation you feel when you don't
Numismatics	Collecting money for fun

–O–

OK	"Yes" in two words
Octogenarian	A man who makes the same mistake he did at seventy
Old age	When all the girls look alike to you
Oleomargarine	Something you have to take for butter or worse
Optimist	A person who says the bottle is half full when it's half empty
Ostrich	The giraffe among birds

Ouch!	The class yell of experience
Overeating	An activity that will make you thick to your stomach
Oyster stew	A food in which you sometimes find a pearl but rarely an oyster

–P–

P	A letter that's always in "peace"
Pancake	It always has to wait its turn
Pandemonium	A din of iniquity
Pillow	A nap sack
Plagiarist	A man whose scissors are sharper than his wits
Play	Work you don't have to do
Police station	A place where sleeping is all right in a pinch
Political plum	The result of careful grafting
Postman	The man from whom all the girls get love letters
Pretzel	A biscuit on a bender
Prisoner	A bird in a guilty cage
Profanity	The father tongue
Prophet	A person who foresees trouble

–R–

RSVP	Refreshments Served Very Promptly
Rug	A bedspread for people who sleep on the floor

Rumor	A monster with more tales than an octopus
Rush hour	When traffic is at a standstill
Rumba	Waving goodbye without using your hand

–S–

S	A letter that's shaped like a snake because it hisses
Sable	The skin girls love to touch
Safe bet	The one you were going to make but didn't
Saint Bernard dog	A dog with a liquor license
Salisbury steak	Hamburger at a higher price
Salt	Something useful in a pinch
Sarong	A bath towel that made good
Scalp	Something that is hair today and gone tomorrow
Scissors	A piece maker
Senile	What a man is when he watches the food instead of the waitress
Siamese twins	First person plural
Sin	What every girl should "no"
Skeleton	A joint concern
Slacker	A woman who wears slacks
Slot machine	Something that makes money without working

–T–

T	The difference between here and there
Tact	Social lying
Tail	Something attached behind the behind
Termite	Termites are boring. They work with all termite.
Thirty	A nice age for a woman especially if she is forty
Thongs	What Thinatra things
Thumb	The thick finger on the hand of a woman that usually has a man under it
Timekeeper	A clock-eyed man
Toast	The only thing that can be eaten or drunk
Travel folder	A trip tease
Trojan horse	A phony pony
Turkish bath	A pool room
Twice-told tale	A story that's been told a thousand times
Typographical error	A misprint that can turn a hat into a cat and a baby sitter into a baby sister

–U–

Umbrella	A portable roof when it rains
University	A college with a stadium seating more than sixty thousand
Unskilled labor	Found mostly in professions

Upper hand	Something not found in a friendly handshake
Useless	The things we ought to use less, or a glass eye at a keyhole

–V–

Varicose veins	Very close veins
Venom	Doing with your tongue what you haven't enough courage to do with your hands
Ventriloquist	A man with a dummy who always talks to himself
Venus	The girl who got the breaks
Village	A small town where everybody knows the troubles you've seen
Virus	A Latin term meaning "Your guess is as good as mine"
Vision	What people think you have when you guess right
Vote	To choose the lesser of two evils

–W–

Waffle	A pancake with a nonskid tread
Wallflower	A decoration for ballrooms
Wall Street	The capital of capital
Warden	A man who makes his living by his pen
Watchmaker	A man who has lots of time on his hands
Waterfall	A drop of water

Wedlock	A padlock
Western	A sage saga
Will power	Eating only one peanut
Window	A looking-out glass
Wink	A whether signal
Wrinkle	Yesterday's dimple

–X–

X-ray	A ray that enables a person to see through anything except treachery
Xylophonist	A superstitious person who goes around knocking on wood

–Y–

Yacht	A floating debt
Yawn	A hole made by a bore
Year	A period of 365 disappointments
Yeast	A good razor
Yellow journalism	Something sensational that is always read
Yes-man	One who stoops to concur
Yesterday	The tomorrow that got away
Yours truly	The last letter in the English language

–Z–

Zebra	A horse with stripes

Zigzag	The shortest distance between two drinks
Zither	A lap harp
Zygmurgy	The last word according to Funk and Wagnall

A-PUN-dix

One of the best pun pals I know is my number one son, Stan, who heads SFM Entertainment, New York, and is a great entrepreneur. He includes among his pastimes visiting nursing and rest homes to help encourage the occupants to play "connect the liver spots on the backs of their hands." His list of daffynitions include the following:

Alarm Clock A small device used to wake up people who have no children

Bigamist A man who leads two wives

Coward One who in a perilous emergency thinks with his legs

Diamond	A chunk of coal that made good under pressure
Education	Something a person spends years getting so he can work for another person who has no education at all
Flirtation	Wishful winking
Genius	The talent of a man who is dead
Hollywood	Where you put on a sports jacket and take off your brain
IOU	A paper wait
Janitor	A floor flusher
Kleptomaniac	One who helps himself because he can't help himself
Lonely person	A guy who can't admit that he finds himself poor company
Marriage	A kind of friendship that is recognized by the church
Nudists	Folks who grin and bare it
Overeating	The destiny that shapes our ends
Philosophy	Unintelligible answers to insoluble problems
Religion	Insurance in this world against a fire in the next
Spinster	A woman who is unhappily unmarried
Television	Chewing gum for the eyes
Undertaker	The last guy to let you down
Vocabulary	Something a man can use to describe a shapely girl without using his hands
Writers	Writers are born, not paid
Yawn	A silence with an exclamation mark
Zoo	A place where animals look at silly people

Credits

At the outset, I would like to take this opportunity to express my gratitude and appreciation to all the punsters and pundits who have taken interest and made the effort to share their favorite puns with me and you. Unfortunately, I cannot list individual credits to all the contributors due to the difficulty in determining the puns' sources and originality. Where possible, I have listed some names of those who sent me puns or told them to me. Without your help this book would have been much smaller and less interesting.

Some credits, where credits are due: "For Better or Worse: The Pun Never Sets on Britain's Empire" by Alan L. Otten © 1987, Dow Jones, Incorporated (The Wall Street Journal); "Ziggy" cartoon © 1987 Universal Press Syndicate; Introduction by Bob Hope; "B.C."

Credits